Man's Concern With Holiness

MAN'S CONCERN WITH HOLINESS

edited by
MARINA CHAVCHAVADZE

with contributions by

Geoffrey Curtis C. R.
Monica Furlong
A. M. Allchin
Geddes MacGregor
Philip Caraman S. J.
Regin Prenter
Paul Evdokimov

HODDER AND STOUGHTON

SBN   340   10575 5

Acknowledgements

T. S. Eliot's *Murder in the Cathedral* and 'Little Gidding', from *Collected Poems, 1909-1962*, are quoted by permission of Faber and Faber Ltd.; Gerard Manley Hopkins' 'Thee, God, I come from' and 'Inversaid', from the *Collected Poems*, are quoted by permission of the Oxford University Press.

Printed in Great Britain for Hodder and Stoughton, Ltd.,
Saint Paul's House, Warwick Lane, London, E.C.4. by
T. & A. Constable Ltd., Hopetoun Street, Edinburgh EH7 4NF

Contents

Love takes to itself the life of the loved one.
The greater the love, the greater the suffering of the soul.
The fuller the love, the fuller the knowledge of God.
The more ardent the love, the more fervent the prayer.
The more perfect the love, the holier the life.

From the writings of Starets Silouan
(*The Undistorted Image*,
by Archimandrite Sophrony, Faith Press)

Editor's Foreword

At the heart of all great religions is a deep concern with holiness. These ancient faiths have influenced men's behaviour and fostered spiritual growth down the ages but, in the final count, it is Christ, *The Holy One*, who stands as the supreme revelation of holiness.

This book sets out not only to present sanctified lives but to examine various aspects of wholeness or holiness as it evolved within Christianity. The main differing traditions of holiness are described here by specialists in these fields which also include Methodism, the Society of Friends, Pentacostalism, the Salvation Army, Congregationalism, and Baptist movements. Though not a comparative study, this book presents an alignment of spiritualities from pragmatic holiness to mysticism, which stimulates essential comparisons.

It is hoped that this work will make a contribution towards unity and a deeper understanding among Christians by shewing the indwelling of God's Spirit within each of these separate traditions. At present the theological differences appear insurmountable, for, in the words of our Lord, we neglect the commandment of God, in order to maintain the tradition of man (Mark 7.8 N.E.B.) and we see how theology without holy love can only encompass the intellectual ingredients of truth; it cannot serve as an instrument of peace. When John XXIII used his authority to recall the world to the obligation of love, a bright ray of hope shone throughout Christendom because even the man in the street recognised in him the twofold stamp of humanity and holiness. Today hope lingers over the ecumenical dialogues and flares sporadically over the great evangelical crusades, but it is in the small, nameless groups of people meeting in prayer, and in the communities which await His coming, that we find a steadfast advance towards holiness. This silent activity is opening up a new era of communication and spiritual power throughout the world, especially where the persecuted churches are being consecrated by the blood of their martyrs.

The agonised cry of St. Joan in the final act of Shaw's play, is the voice of our century: "When, when, O God, will the earth be ready for your saints?"

*   *   *

Man's concern with holiness is expressing itself today in many ways – revival of interest in the Gospel, baptism of the Spirit, tongues, new theologies, ecumenical dialogues, communities of prayer, healing. It is on this last manifestation that I should like to make some comment because I brought this book together as Editor through my involvement in a centre for spiritual and medical healing, where I discovered that holiness and healing are closely related. The idea took shape over the years through meeting people of all faiths, denominations and nationalities who come enquiring about prayer and healing. They have taught me to realise that the living Christ responds to every prayer, especially prayer offered up in pain, grief, rejection, or situations of humiliating dependence, which deepen and refine our receptivity to God; that such suffering ceases to be destructive but becomes a transforming power. In what Iulia de Beausobre calls "the node where God and man meet" the mystery of the Cross is finally resolved and the first steps towards holiness are taken.

On another level I also discovered how puzzled people are by the widespread manifestations of psychic phenomena and how many mistake them for the miraculous. Most of our authors have written about the supernatural within their traditions but it may be useful to consider briefly the vocation of men and women who exercise healing powers in our time.

The question is often asked: can healers and preachers with prophetic missions claim holiness on account of their good works? The number of faith healers and spiritual healers in the world today has grown into many thousands and the difference that exists between them and those who are endowed with charismatic or supernatural gifts, is ill-defined. The former draw their powers from realms of the mind or soul, the nature of which is psychic. Charismatics are relatively rare and act under direct obedience to the Holy Spirit, preferring to call their ministry *Divine* healing, and many of these bear a close resemblance to the saints. It is impossible to make a clear-cut distinction between the two categories of healers because most possess an admixture of gifts both natural and supernatural. Since there exists a divergence between character and gifts, personal standards of behaviour are more reliable criteria of holiness than the possession of miraculous powers or a capacity for visions.

To understand Christian sanctity this book must be read in its entirety. It includes most aspects except the reverse side of the coin – counterfeit holiness. False spirituality lies beyond the scope of this work, but we should consider it briefly because Jesus attached such importance to it and because it is increasing in the world today in many guises. He gave a solemn warning about this danger, "Beware of false prophets, men who come to you dressed up as sheep while underneath they are savage wolves." (Matt. 7.15 N.E.B.)

Good gifts in evil men have always caused perplexity, and Oswald Chambers, the great Baptist preacher, wrote forcibly on this subject in his *Biblical Ethics*: "God will honour His words whether a saint or a bad man preaches it; this is one of the startling things that our Lord says." He is referring to Matthew 7.21-23 where men and women claim salvation because they have prophesied, cast out demons and worked miracles in the name of Jesus. The Lord, however, tells them, "I never knew you; out of my sight, you and your wicked ways!" This apparent contradiction is weighted with unanswered questions but it suggests that some healers and preachers take up this work without a true vocation, or, having begun their calling in obedience to God, they ultimately become corrupted like Judas. Involvement in spiritual and psychic activities is hazardous for all, and many who practise these gifts have lost their way, but for the Christian there is perfect safety in remaining anchored to Christ.

Although discernment is a gift of the Spirit, Jesus lays this responsibility on us all: if we love Him enough we shall not be deceived. In His words, the shepherd "calls his own sheep by name . . . and the sheep follow because they know his voice. They will not follow a stranger." And St. John writes, "do not trust any and every spirit, my friends; test the spirits, to see whether they are from God". (1 John 4.1 N.E.B.) This puts us on our guard to distinguish between spiritual, psychic and demonic forces. Christ's reply to His disciples' questions about false prophets holds good for all time. "You will recognise them by the fruits they bear . . . a good tree always yields good fruit, and a poor tree bad fruit." (Matt. 7.16-17 N.E.B.)

Genuine holiness is, therefore, proved by the nature of the tree and its fruits. In his first letter to the Corinthians (ch.13) St. Paul designates the tree as love, and in his hymn of praise of charity he describes the character of Jesus. "Love is never boastful, nor conceited, nor rude . . . does not gloat over men's sins, but delights in the truth. There is nothing love cannot face; there is no limit to its faith, its hope, its endurance. Love will never come to an end."

*   *   *

Before mentioning all who have made this book possible I must first express my very special gratitude to Dr. Eric Abbott for his unfailing support and advice, also to Miss Dorothy Musgrave Arnold, without whose encouragement this book could never have been completed.

On the editorial side I am especially indebted to Dr. Jean Young for the time she has given and for her scholarly advice, equally for undertaking to compile the Index. My thanks are due to Miss Eileen Corrigan for reading the manuscripts, and to Mr. Peter Armstrong of Mansfield College, Oxford, who did expert editing of the Lutheran study. I am also very grateful to Miss Constance Babington Smith for undertaking the translation of *Holiness in The Orthodox Tradition*.

When I first made enquiries about whom I should ask to be contributors, much useful advice and help was given me. Among these many kind responses, I am especially indebted to the Very Reverend Archimandrite Sophrony, Abbot of the Stavropedic Orthodox Monastery of St. John the Baptist in Essex, to the Right Reverend Oliver Tomkin, Bishop of Bristol, the Reverend Canon J. R. Satterthwaite of the Council of Foreign Relations, Lambeth, and to the Reverend Patrick Rodger of the World Council of Churches in Geneva.

I cannot conclude without a word about my publishers. My special appreciation goes to Mr. Leonard Cutts for inviting me to undertake this work, and to Mr. Robin Denniston for his encouragement and patience over the three years of editorial preparation.

Burrswood   Marina Chavchavadze
Groombridge
Kent

Introduction

by

GEOFFREY CURTIS C.R.

Geoffrey Curtis, B.A., C.R., was born in 1902 in London. He was a classical scholar at Charterhouse and from there won an open scholarship to University College, Oxford. After two years at Cuddesdon College, Oxford, he was ordained to the sacred ministry. He became a member of the Community of the Resurrection where, especially as lecturer and tutor for over twenty years in the theological college which it serves, he has done much teaching. Father Curtis is also known all over the world as an ecumenist. His books include: *William of Glasshampton, Friar, Monk Solitary*, 1947; *Paul Couturier and Unity in Christ*, 1963.

"HOLINESS," said Nathan Söderblom, Archbishop of Uppsala, the great forefather of the World Council of Churches, "is the great word in religion; it is even more essential than the notion of God. Real religion may exist without a definite conception of divinity, but there is no real religion without a distinction between holy and profane. The attaching of undue importance to the conception of divinity has often led to the exclusion from the realm of religion of (1) phenomena at the primitive stage as being magic, though they are characteristically religious: and of (2) Buddhism and other higher forms of salvation and piety which do not involve a belief in God. The only sure test is holiness. From the first, holiness constitutes the most essential feature of the divine in a religious sense."[1]

Three comments may be made on this identification of religion with a sense of holiness. First, if this is true, it is not surprising that the ecumenical movement of the Christian Churches has found itself confronting serious and perhaps insurmountable obstacles in its quest of unity in Christ, since its members have concentrated on the necessity of doctrinal and structural oneness amongst the churches rather than on the need of union in the element which in early centuries was the first to win expression and draw veneration – essential holiness. Secondly, it is hardly strange that this movement has been characterised by introversion and has shown comparatively little sign of desiring to find points of union with other religions or of labouring for the unity of all mankind. Thirdly, it is natural that an age which ignores the notion of holiness, should be delighted with the idea of "religionless Christianity": and this in a very different sense from that in which the holy servant of God, Bonhoeffer, coined the phrase "religionless Christianity", meaning thereby to denote the Christian life as "being for others" – a "complete and joyous openness to the whole multifarious world around him" made possible for the Christian by a "secret discipline" which includes prayer, meditation, common worship, sacraments and experiments in "life together".[2]

[1] Archbishop Nathan Söderblom: "Holiness, general and primitive" in Hastings *Encyclopaedia of Religion and Ethics*. Vol. VI, pp. 731-41.
[2] "The isolated use and handing down of the famous term 'religionless Christianity' has made Bonhoeffer the champion of an undialectical shallow modernism which obscures all that he wanted to tell us about the living God." (Eberhard Bethge in a lecture entitled "The Living God Revealed in His Church", delivered in Coventry Cathedral, Oct. 30, 1967.)

What do we mean by holiness? The concept of holiness in the Bible has a background shared with other ancient religions. That which is holy is set apart, reserved for habitation or use by the divine or for religious operation by man in contrast to what is common or profane. The notion of holiness in scripture is soon transformed as it is disclosed that the Holy is pre-eminently God Himself, so that holiness is the otherness, the separateness, the distinctiveness of the God of righteousness. But let us keep for a moment to the territory common to all the great religions. Rudolf Otto in his great book *The Idea of the Holy* draws attention to two notable features of holiness. First there is the element of awefulness, disconcertingness, paralysing stupor. This aspect of the holy, notable in Hebraic as well as in other kinds of religious experience, Otto calls the *numinous*. Thus experienced, the holy is known as *mysterium tremendum*. But it is not only *tremendum*, daunting, it is also *fascinans*.

"For the sense of the holy," Otto writes, "appears as the sense of something that commands incomparable respect, something in which one must recognise supreme objective value. Awe in the presence of divine holiness does not coincide with mere dread of absolute power, in face of which no other attitude is possible than that of blind and abject obedience. 'Thou only art holy' is not the cry of fear, but a salutation of praise overflowing with veneration; it is not the mere stammering of man in the presence of one who represents superior power, it is the sentence in which man desires to recognise and exalt that which possesses a value beyond his comprehension. What he exalts is . . . the power which deserves to be served, because it is worthy of the highest service."[1]

Thus holiness from the first evokes a judgement of value and a sense of responsibility. The awe which it elicits draws forth at the same time reverence which finds expression in ethical relationships. So it was between Israel, the elect race, the holy nation and her God. She was a holy people, distinct and separate from the world because chosen by the only holy God. This gave Israel a status the meaning of which she was perpetually tempted to misunderstand. It proved possible, paradoxically enough, to interpret such a status in a direction completely contrary to its true purport – in terms of privilege, aloofness, superiority rather than as entailing specially and confessedly unique dependence upon God. It could be interpreted in terms of enjoying superior religious practices and of being secure if these were correctly performed. There were certainly

[1] Rudolf Otto. *The Idea of the Holy*. Fr. John V. Harvey (O.U.P., 1924, p. 53f.), quoted but differently translated by Michael Ramsey, Archbishop of Canterbury, in his address: "The Idea of the Holy and the World Today", in *Spirituality for Today*, Eric James, S.C.M., 1968.

centuries during which Israel saw her calling thus in terms of superiority and insulation from other nations and from the world. But whenever she succumbed to these temptations, she found that her holiness, so far from protecting her from the scathing judgements of God seemed rather to expose her to them and draw them upon her so that she might learn that her holiness which was grounded in God's choice of her, required her to do justly, to have mercy and to walk humbly before God – and that her uniqueness must find expression in the service of the human race whose priest and servant she was called to be.[1]

The outgoing movement of the holy God towards men found its climax in Jesus the chosen one of God, the Son of Man who alone realised perfectly the dependence of Israel and of all mankind on God for cleansing and mission. He alone wholly emptied of self-will is the perfect receptacle and organ of the Holy Spirit of God. In His life among the chosen people in Palestine the notes of holiness find unique expression. The compassion which drew such crowds to Him was coupled with power that struck with awe those who saw and heard Him. How full the Gospels are, especially the Marcan proclamation of Jesus as the crucified Messiah, of wonder, joy, astonishment, fear and trembling. "And they were in the way going up to Jerusalem and Jesus was going before them. And they were amazed and they that followed were afraid." (Mark 10.32) Jesus the anointed of the Spirit of holiness, though wholly, indeed uniquely human, is as certainly "other, different, shocking, lonely".

The radiant life-giving ministry of Galilee is succeeded by the stormy *chiaroscuro* of the final ministry in Jerusalem. After the lonely death comes following swiftly upon it, the mingled joy and terror of Easter morning when the women flee from the tomb "for they were beside themselves with terror. They said nothing to anybody for they were afraid." (Mark 16.8 N.E.B.) Awe shot though by fascination – the two elements of the numinous are strikingly close to one another in the Gospel records and are found wonderfully united in the Transfiguration. "The disciples are awestruck, but they find it good to be there and they want to be nowhere else."[2]

Through the whole story of the life and passion of the Christ there has appeared a new revelation of the meaning of holiness. The aweful yet winsome mystery of divine being is made known as the mystery of self-giving love, unutterable in words yet spelt out thus at Bethlehem, in the upper room, in Gethsemane and on Calvary. The holy in terms

---

[1] Ramsey, *op. cit.*   [2] *Ibid.*

of love human and divine finds its most perfect expression in language in the Lord's own eucharistic prayer of self-consecration in the seventeenth chapter of Saint John. "Holy Father" – so Jesus names God here – "protect by the power of thine own name those whom thou hast given me so that they may be one as we are one" (John 17.11 N.E.B.) and He speaks of Himself as for the sake of His followers "consecrating (sanctifying) Himself so that they may be consecrated (sanctified) in the truth". This wondrous interchange of love in truth with God and those who are His, is, He makes clear, ever rendered luminous in the world by *glory* – the other great correlative of holiness. (John 17.22) The glory of God, the dazzling splendour, majesty and beauty of God – Jesus reveals its essence in the wondrous radiance of self-giving love. Here the divine otherness is made visible as rendering itself truly one with the world, its essence being to give and to serve; yet it remains clearly other, as having no created source and though it draws upon itself the world's shame, evoking wonder and praise from the pure in heart. The divine glory of self-forgetful self-spending love is found again and again in crucial conflict with the human glory of pride and self-aggrandisement. Men crucified Jesus because "they loved the glory of man more than the glory of God". (John 12.43)

But through the triumph of holy love, the resurrection of Jesus, there was raised for Him from the dead God's holy people, the Israel of God. It consisted of those who accepted the Messiahship of the crucified, risen and glorified Jesus and who thereby receiving His spirit became members of His body the Church of God. The Holy Spirit reproduces in the Christian community the holiness which Jesus embodied and which He revealed as humble self-giving charity. The life resultant from this is concerned not in the first place with ethics and altruism, the love and service of man. There is a godward reference and perspective in holiness which makes it "an uncomfortable word in the modern world". Many an upright and virtuous life is devoid of holiness. Many a life is holy despite obvious moral blemishes and failings.

The articles collected in this book make clear enough that holiness is the note on which the churches are in closest concord. This must needs be so because their holiness, however varied in the emphasis of each, cannot be other than the holiness of Christ. As to unity, disunited as they are amongst themselves even their ideals of unity must have a less unquestionable origin than has their holiness. You will find great variety certainly in these notions of sanctity and many surprises. Who would have guessed that there is in English spirituality 'a profound if hidden affinity with Eastern Orthodoxy'? That it is the Reformed or Calvinist protestant tradition which stresses most the merriment of the saints? That the most compelling words cited as to the value of continous contemplation – prayer at all times – are not those of a monk of Mount Athos or of some western anchoress but of the Reformer, Martin Luther? That the Roman Catholic contribution, while entirely destitute of any juridicial note, should be a concise inspiring apotheosis of holiness as charity, of charity perfected in suffering through the indwelling Christ? That the Eastern Orthodox tradition should be large enough to englobe all these lights and yet in cosmic perspective to transfigure all with radiance from above? The Eastern Orthodox contribution is larger than that of any other writer. But then this subject has taken a first place in the doctrine of the Holy Orthodox Church. Here the door into heaven thrown open by the Resurrection of Christ has been kept always open: to attend the Eastern liturgy is to share the worship of the saints. The light that shines through ikons has a numinous quality, radiant and awesome. A young English agnostic, translator of Freud's monograph on religion, *The Future of an Illusion,* was so moved by the exhibition of ikons held in London after the Bolshevik revolution that the cold light of reason and scientific analysis never afterwards fully satisfied him.

The positive notes struck by each contributor – gospel notes which would be welcomed by all as enriching the whole symphony – are of course more valuable than those which spring from the special historical heritage of each. Nevertheless there are vital points in the Christian notion of holiness untouched by the ecumenical contributors to this symposium. That is why it is so good to have Monica Furlong's challenging expression of the attitude of the modern age. Other points I have noted which need further discussion.

(1) In holiness – the quest and apprehension of the Holy – is found the Christian's point of union with the other religions. Until we realise and explore this there is no hope of our realising the vision of a wider ecumenical movement for all men of good will, moving outwards from the ecumenical movement in the Christian Churches to the service of and cooperation with men of other faiths, finally to the succour of all mankind.

(2) There has been a disastrous hardening of the distinction between the sacred and the secular into a real separation, a dichotomy; that

B

barrier which the incarnation of God *ipso facto* abolished. This has been due to a deeper more fatal error – the idea that man can by his own efforts become holy. The words "called to be saints" to be found in classic English translations at the opening of the Pauline letters, if not a mistranslation, are at least patient of fatal misunderstanding. The words really indicate that the readers are holy by calling, called in holiness. Man can never become holy by his own effort; Christians are those who realise this from the start. We, the baptised, are holy because we have been chosen and called by the Holy God. It is our business to become what we are. To identify with holiness the area of life which belongs to professional religious practice – holy books, holy buildings, holy feelings, etc. – is to do worse than short-circuit this energy of God. To make it rest in these things without flowing forth into the world of His redemption is to dechristianise as well as to dehumanise the holiness of the Church. In our era at least, as Dag Hammarskjöld has noted, the road of holiness "passes necessarily through the world of action".

(3) There is a fatal failure nowadays to realise that science and all its triumphs in technology are themselves products of the dedication of mind to the pursuit of truth with regard to the material world, a disposition which was itself a by-product of the Christian faith. These achievements may indeed be called miraculous fruits of a special kind of holiness: miraculous because miracle is not as it has often been thought to be the violation of scientific law – there are ultimately no laws that are not grounded in the truth of the divine being – but that which evokes godly wonder. It is, as has been said, a fallacy to find more of God in the special than in the general, for example in a healing by laying-on-of-hands than in a healing by surgery. "God is just as much at work and just as wonderingly to be praised in the techniques which man has mastered as in the processes which remain a mystery to him," writes Rev. John V. Taylor.[1]

What is surely desirable is the harmonious combination of both kinds of awareness and service. For instance, as a modern example of science and faith working together, the Dorothy Kerin Home of Healing at Burrswood is a place where the wind of miracle blows; but where it would seem ludicrous to regard God's answers to prayer or to the touch of healing hands in the sanctuary as more His own or as having a greater claim for gratitude than the cures due to the skilled devotion of doctors and nurses and their special knowledge and art. It is scientifically

[1] *C. M. S. Letters*, 1968.

impossible to isolate the results of one kind of service from those of the other. It is true that an instantaneous miraculous healing though the laying-on-of-hands or sacraments is a more striking response from God to prayer; but the primary miracle which is to be wonderingly appraised is that of charity, the divine human love operative in so many complementary ways. All this varied endeavour at Burrswood is due ultimately to one particular life which bore eminently the marks of holiness. Dorothy Kerin's faith in God energising through the indwelling Christ flowed forth in loving, joyous, sacrificial service of others and was rewarded by fruit both supernatural and natural. Dorothy Kerin's life itself is specially marked out as being a whole-hearted response to the miraculous act of God in restoring her from the jaws of death. It is true that all genuine holiness has this character of being a response to the wonderful kindness of God. But this life stands out, a vivid sign or type of the givenness of holy living in our century, having led not only to fresh insight into the harmony between science and religious faith, but to the expression of this in the new pattern of therapy.

Dorothy Kerin's miraculous healing and ministry did bring to many doctors, by their own admission, a fresh insight into God's healing power. The story of her healing in 1912 is well known.[1] Dorothy had been ailing for years and had come to the point where her death was considered to be imminent. She was diagnosed as suffering from tubercular meningitis, peritonitis, diabetes and other complications. She was being fed by injections and was too weak to lift her hands. At length she was pronounced to be dying. She received Holy Communion on the Sunday morning and the same evening passed into a mystical experience during which a voice called her by name three times and told her that her sufferings were over and that she was to get up and walk. She had not walked for over five years, but she now got up and walked quite steadily, to the astonishment and alarm of her mother and friends gathered round the bed. Then feeling hungry she dismissed invalid food and went downstairs to the larder, returning with some meat and pudding which she ate without pain or discomfort – the first solid food that she had been able to digest for years. Overnight she was restored from an emaciated condition to the well-covered normal body of a healthy girl. Dorothy Kerin was raised up from the brink of death because she had a great vocation to fulfil. Her life work culminated in the establishment of the Home of Healing at Burrswood which has been a factor of no little importance in the restoration of the healing ministry

[1] *The Living Touch*, by Dorothy Kerin. Hodder & Stoughton.

of Christ in the Church of our day and in the growth of true Christian holiness.

Holiness in human life means consecration to God in Whose image we are made. In so far as it does find moral expression in human character, it will not find expression chiefly in deference, passivity, quietude. It does involve primarily the courage to be ourselves. This entails self-forgetful love towards God and others and consequent joy in living. The opposite to holiness is not pride, which has so long been allowed to take rank as the sin of sins, but sloth: sloth understood to mean "being less than instead of more than man". The Greek word which we often use the word sloth to translate, *acedia*, comes from the Greek words not caring (*a*=not: *Kedos*=care). Caring, as Baron Von Hügel insisted to his niece, is what matters most in life. "Sloth,' remarks Joseph Pieper, "does not mean mere idleness, rather it means that man renounces the claim implicit in his human dignity," or as Harvey Cox paraphrases, "does not wish to be what he fundamentally and really is".[1]

Cardinal Suhard, spiritual father of the French worker-priest movement, once said that it is not the task of Christians to advocate a programme or ideology, but rather to create a mystery that cannot be explained by any human thinking and can finally only be understood as the grace of God. Could not the vital truth here hinted be given more careful expression? There is no need to "create a mystery", for it is already there. We do not need to discover it. For the mystery is *mysterium fidei*, the mystery of Christ to Whom we belong. Our need is rather to be more truly involved in Him so as to liberate His living energy to complete the work of setting the world free. Overthrowing the false image of holiness and learning to be ourselves we shall be the first to know that freedom. Perhaps this is what Julia Howe meant in the haunting words:

> In the beauty of the lilies Christ was born across the sea
> With a glory in his bosom that transfigures you and me.
> As he died to make men holy, let us die to make men free
>   While God is marching on.

[1] Kierkegaard, Emmanuel Mounier (*viz. The Spoil of the Violent*, tr. K. Watson. Havill Press, 1955) and Joseph Pieper (*Leisure, the Basis of Culture*, Faber, 1952) have all seen this: Harvey Cox has given more recent and powerful expression to the point in the book commended below.

In so doing we shall find that the two purposes spoken of in the third line, His and ours – the quest for holiness and that for freedom – are one and the same; so that our intention is one with His in the divine humanism of the carpenter, the holy one of Nazareth.

.   .   .

I am deeply indebted to ✠ Michael, Archbishop of Canterbury, one of the few theologians who realise that the epoch opened by Doctor Rudolf Otto's great book, *The Idea of the Holy*, has not passed, though it has been shamefully bypassed. See in particular Archbishop Ramsey's address, "The Idea of the Holy and the World Today", in *Spirituality for Today*, ed. Eric James, S.C.M., 1968. I owe also much to a brilliant book by Harvey G. Cox – *On Not Leaving It to the Snake*, S.C.M., 1968. Both these writings I have pillaged in the hope of whetting appetites for their perusal. I should like also to call attention to the outstanding scriptural passage on this subject from the Decree on the Church (*Lumen Gentium*) issued by the Second Vatican Council. This constitutes the fifth chapter of this decree and is entitled *The Call of the Whole Church to Holiness*.

Holiness
in
The Continuing Tradition

by

Monica Furlong

Monica Furlong was born in Harrow in 1930. She has written on religious affairs for the *Spectator* and *The Guardian*; was a columnist on the *Daily Mail* for six years; and wrote her first book, *With Love to the Church*, in 1965, in which she voiced fundamental objections to modern churchianity. Miss Furlong now lives in Ruislip, Middlesex with her husband and two children.

The subject of holiness produces in me an obscure distress, like that of the snobbish heroine who detected a pea under the mattress. There is a suggestion of an élite about it which sits uneasily in the twentieth century: I sympathise deeply with a friend of mine who objected bitterly, after seeing *The Cocktail Party*, that while the saint Celia enjoyed all the drama of martyrdom, all that was permitted to poor Edward and Lavinia was "the stale food mouldering in the larder, the stale thoughts mouldering in their minds. Each unable to disguise his own meanness from himself, because it is known to the other." Not a cheerful future, and scarcely what the New Testament seems to promise. For if one is going to have an aristocracy of goodness, then this seems to imply the need for its opposite, a rabble of *sans culottes*. And looking back over the Church's history it would not be difficult to find periods when the prevailing consciousness has been precisely of this huge and unbridgeable gulf between the saints and others.

Does it matter? Talking of a similar cult, the cult of the hero, Brecht makes one of his characters exclaim "Unhappy is the land that needs a hero" and there is a sense in which one might adapt this as "Unhappy is the church that needs a saint". For, too easily nation, or church, caught in the grip of herd emotion, projects such unconscious images upon individuals, and becomes blind to the realities of the situation. The reality of the situation – of every situation – is that each individual is called upon to realise his own goodness, his own courage (and, the Jungians would say, his own shadow side) and not to push it outwards upon some public champion or scapegoat. For such mass projections not only turn individuals into a blind and clumsy herd, but reduce the object of their attentions to a puppet, helpless and drained of humanity. So often things written and said about Christian saints have achieved just this kind of damaging projection. They were presented as independent of physical laws (they could go without food, they were not subject to gravity, their bodies did not decay after death, and when they were martyred their bodies gave off a sweet smell). And they were equally independent of psychological laws – they were never depressed, bored, sexually frustrated, bad-tempered, self-pitying, prejudiced, or a bore to their nearest and dearest, like you and me.

Fortunately, side by side with this inflated version of sanctity there has been another tradition which has insisted upon, and relished, the humanity of the saint. In *The Brothers Karamazov* Dostoïevsky paints a wryly amusing picture of the scene when the good Fr. Zossima dies. His friends and disciples are determined that, true to the tradition of sanctity, his body shall not decay in death. Some of his fellow-monks, however, who feel his reputation is undeserved (he has a weakness for taking tea and cherry jam, and in the company of ladies), feel that at last he will be exposed as a non-runner in the sanctity stakes. And sure enough, after three days of warmish weather, it begins to be apparent to even the most idealistic disciple that Fr. Zossima's body is going the way of mortality. Dostoievsky leaves us to draw the moral – that it is the fruits of Zossima's life which must define him, and not the trivia of his death.

In a curious way the decay of his body in death stamps him as a great and holy man just as surely as his wonderful love for people, his power over sickness, or the utter simplicity of his life. He is ordinary. He is one of us. In his time he has felt hunger and thirst, heat and cold, sickness and health, exhaustion and energy, just as we do. He has known fear, anxiety, anger, guilt, sexual desire, joy, hope, ambition – all the constellations which go to make up our daily struggle with life. In death he stinks. In short he is not a god come among men, however much it would suit us to think so. He is our own very ordinary clay beautifully transformed.

The nature of this transformation is what I am attempting to discuss in this chapter, but before I go any further I want to mention what it is that strikes me over and over again about sanctity, both in its major manifestations, and in the smaller degrees in which we see seeds of it in practically everyone we know – that it is, above all, ordinary, that it is ordinariness so much loved and treasured, so much polished and cherished, that it becomes extraordinary. And if ordinariness is the hallmark of goodness, then it is in ordinary ways that we tend to discover it; the simple, undefended remark that comes from the heart, or the humdrum gesture, like passing the salt, which indicates a long habit of living as if other selves are as important as oneself. It is moments like these, much more than great dramas of martyrdom, which illuminate the lives of the rest of us, showing us not only the way we have to travel to learn the art of goodness, but also, paradoxically, how close and easy it all is. We do not want it to be easy. In our blindness and folly, we want elaboration and complexity, we want the pomp of heroism, the thrill of masochism, the glittering prize of perfection at the end of an arduous journey. What we do not want is to give up having a role. We want to make something of ourselves. We want, narcissistically, to catch ourselves doing something we like the look of. "One must abandon every attempt to make something of oneself," wrote Bonhoeffer "whether it be a saint, a converted sinner, a churchman . . . a righteous man or an unrighteous one."

Bonhoeffer was pleading for a new sort of unselfconsciousness in the Christian. He felt he should be so steeped in the struggle of everyday existence, with its duties and problems, its successes and failures, its experiences and helplessness, that he had no time or energy to watch himself doing it. "It is in such a life that we throw ourselves utterly into the arms of God and participate in His sufferings in the world."

For Bonhoeffer, the Christian achievement was "to be a man, pure and simple, as Jesus was a man." He seemed to feel that this was incompatible with sanctity. Perhaps, however, it *is* sanctity, and one aspect of sanctity is the total unselfconsciousness of the principal actor. Bishop Edward King suggested that "really good people are generally a great deal better than they know how to be; they are not conscious at all of being what they are. They are simply what they are, good people, and so they are surprised when the result of their lives at all comes out into view."

Alongside the ordinariness and the unselfconsciousness of the saint, and perhaps emerging from it, is a quality of unexpectedness which nevertheless seems to have a delightful rightness about it. When Pope John invited his gardener in to share his lunch, visited the prisoners in Regina Coeli, or threw his arms around Mrs. Kennedy with a joyful cry of "Jacqueline", it somehow never occurred to anyone to suggest that such devices had a publicity value. Here was a simple, spontaneous, and affectionate man behaving with perfect naturalness – it was his very naturalness which passed into legend.

Another kind of unexpectedness which marks the good seems to lie in their need to assert, often in fairly rudimentary ways, the goodness of much that has had to be excluded from their vocation. "Oh what a pity, this celibacy" said the Dutch Bishop Bekkers once, as he swept up a small child in his arms. This remark moves, partly because of its simple honesty, partly because it is an affirmation of what he has not had. It is the remark of a whole man.

In the early stages of the struggle for goodness the Christian appears to suffer a tragic loss — the loss of the spontaneity which marks pagan man, the childlike capacity to claim instant satisfaction for the multiple appetites of a human being, or to express uncontrolled rage or disappointment when satisfactions are denied, temporarily, or permanently. Perhaps one of the marks of a growing holiness is that the spontaneity returns, cleansed of its earlier egotism, creative for all whom it touches. In the novel *The Priest* by the French novelist Beatrix Beck, two young women wrestle with this problem.

" 'There are two things of which I am absolutely certain, I said to Christine. 'And they contradict each other. The priest is spiritually the the most sublime man I have ever known. And on Sunday, without any possible shadow of a doubt, he deliberately passed close by me and brushed me with his sleeve. You can imagine the effect that has had on me.'

'Yes, I'd already noticed,' said Christine. 'He sometimes does things like that. It's not surprising that he gets bawled out by his bishop.'

'Do you think it's just mischievousness on his part, just fun? It must be what they call the wonderful freedom of the children of God. "Love, and do whatever you wish." But me, it knocks me sideways.'

'He does that sort of thing to goad us on,' said Christine. 'But of course it's a risk. He's not frightened, though. He's no more frightened of that than he is of anything else.' "

An action which, at an earlier stage of the priest Morin's development, would have been unpardonably provocative becomes (and is understood by others in the situation to become) a foretaste of the freedom offered to the children of God. The small acts of affection and intimacy which are precious (and necessary) to human beings, but which tend, in the experience of everyday life, to become devalued through the fears, hopes, or cupidity of ourselves and others, are redeemed by holiness into a proper expression of love.

It may be, too, that the movement into goodness creates its own blindness, what appears an almost childlike inability to comprehend external danger or evil, perhaps because the real battle with evil has moved inside the person and the projections of evil upon others have been withdrawn. One thinks of Onuphrius, the very touching little saint in Dumitriu's novel *Incognito* who, when the prisoners, freezing in a Siberian winter, were desperately rubbing themselves against one another, behaved with the "earnest gravity of a child playing a game, a childlike gaiety". Or even nearer to the heart of the matter, the extraordinary incident recorded (among many extraordinary incidents) of the Russian Orthodox nun, Mother Maria Skobtsova, who died at Ravensbruck. "Once at roll call Mother Maria began speaking to a Russian girl and failed to notice an SS woman approaching. The woman called her roughly and struck her face with a leather strap as hard as she could. Mother Maria pretended not to notice and quietly finished her sentence in Russian. The SS woman lost all control and showered blows on her face with the strap, but Mother Maria did not concede her a single glance. She told me afterwards that she was not angry even at the time: 'It was as if she were not standing before me.' "

This incident seems to pose very profound psychological questions about what it is that occurs to the human personality in the phenomenon that is usually called sanctity. It is natural, even necessary, for human beings to respond to a threat, say from freezing, with extreme alarm. The normal response to being struck in the face – one of the most sensitive areas of the body and one to which we are instinctively protective – would be to recoil with pain, to weep, to feel an almost ungovernable anger against the person directing the attack. What has happened to Onuphrius and Mother Maria that they feel none of these normal emotions? Doubtless what has gone to the training of both of them, since both had lived for years as Orthodox religious, was what the Jungians call "suppression" – the purposeful denial of certain satisfactions of the ego (different from unconscious denial, which is repression), a process always accompanied by suffering. Reading accounts of Mother Maria giving away her bread to other prisoners, although herself starving, always cheerful, however cold, hungry or ill, lacking in any hatred for the guards who made life such a misery, always gentle, encouraging, sympathetic towards her infinitely miserable companions, one realises that one is contemplating something beyond goodness or heroism. Some profound change has taken place in this personality. Its centre has moved away from the ego. Survival, both in the physical sense of trying not to let one's body be damaged or destroyed, and in the psychic sense of trying to establish and preserve one's identity among other identities, ceases to be important. It was important once – a proper fulfilment which every human being ought to have – but Mother Maria has reached that point and passed beyond it. It may be arrogance to try to guess what happens next to Mother Maria and others whom we call holy, but the alternative has too often been a rather tiresome mystification which wraps the whole thing in pious jargon and does not seek psychological explanations.

What is striking is how holiness seems invariably to be mixed up with suffering. The subject is either caught up in a cataclysm of suffering which affects others too, like Mother Maria or Martin Luther King, or is the victim of physical illness like Thérèse of Lisieux, or seems withdrawn into some private territory of acute mental suffering which does not appear to be the same thing as the suffering of depressive illness, even when some of the same symptoms are present. What seems to be common in every case is the sense that the subject has chosen the suffering. For some of them, this may not appear to be so – Mother Maria was not free, any more than any other prisoner in Ravensbruck, to choose hunger, cold and brutality – yet there is a sort of freedom there, the freedom of acceptance. This is how things are, and she takes up her position willingly in the centre of it, escaping neither by fantasy nor by aggression. She suffers, and she is helpless except to turn towards the suffering and endure patiently within it. Others find in her serenity and joy.

Is, as Eliot claimed, such suffering a form of action, and if so, what form does the action take? Martin Luther King, after an attempt on his life, five arrests and imprisonments, two bomb attacks on his home, and innumerable threats to his children and his wife, said that he had discovered that suffering was a "creative force". "I have lived these last few years with the conviction that unearned suffering is redemptive."

These two, Mother Maria and Martin Luther King, had seemed to take on, comprehending, extremes of suffering and of evil which thousands of others have had to bear, uncomprehending and without beliefs to help them. They seem, as one studies them, to be voluntarily gazing into the face of evil, entering into combat with it, wrestling with some final secret about opposites which eludes us. The battle with the devil which seemed to be against racialism, or brute force, or sadism, moves out of Ravensbruck or Alabama into the soul, where the adversary is clearly recognisable as the devil. He is no longer alien, but familiar. He has always been known. The soul embarks upon its last transformation, of Gethsemane and Calvary. The opposites are reconciled, the myth (or life-pattern) of man as a fallen being has been changed fundamentally, redemption has occurred. The whole Christian drama has been lived in one patch of humanity. Others are reached and healed by the fact.

In the twentieth century we are bound to scrutinise sanctity with a new knowledge which makes us ask new questions. We look back over the centuries of Christian piety, and find, alongside much courage and love and beauty and joy, things which we can no longer unreservedly admire, nor unquestioningly accept. In the exaggerated fasting, the self-torture, the emphasis on "spiritual" relationships at the expense of ones which found bodily expression, in the longing for pain and martyrdom, we cannot help noting patterns of neurosis and repression which to us spell sickness rather than holiness. What moves one, looking back, is the thought of men, with a primitive psychological understanding, working their way through the infinitely painful processes of discovering their repressions or coming to distrust the masochistic implications of their self-torment. The loneliness of the religious hermit, or the inescapable struggle with other people's characters within the religious community perhaps involved an uncovering of the roots of the personality not unlike that which we associate with psycho-analysis. What clearly happened over and over again was a fundamental change in a man's understanding of himself. As a man progressed in holiness, so the need to visit bizarre forms of self-punishment upon himself ceased, being seen as irrelevant. The agonising struggles with the appetites were seen at length to be frontier skirmishes. Strength was needed for a more fundamental struggle. As they moved towards wholeness (which involved recognising the darkness within instead of punishing it and pushing it out of sight), so they could perceive something of the vast conflict waged unendingly around them; the collision of good and evil.

The conflict itself has not changed over the centuries. What has changed perhaps is the ground where it is fought, and what this in turn demands is a change in the combatants. What holiness means in the twentieth century (but perhaps what it always meant) is a readiness to give oneself up to the conflict, to learn how to enter it. What perhaps is peculiar to our time is that we may have to discover a quite different set of disciplines from the traditional ones if we are to be flexible and wise enough to meet a devil who may not be impressed by fasting.

He has shown himself most hideously in our time in brutal political power and in racialism. It is almost as if the core of evil has moved from the private sector to the public one. It seems to find its expression in mass movements; in millions of Jews being uprooted from their homes and murdered, in other thousands being deliberately starved in Russia to implement Stalin's political policies, in the brutal suppression of the longings of whole nations, such as Hungary and Czechoslovakia, or whole peoples such as black South Africans. Perhaps more insidiously, evil rides us as a kind of mass despair, in which we cry out that life has no meaning, whispering *sotto voce* that we do not intend to find one.

It is when one comes to consider the nature of evil in our time that one must question the value of a spiritual élite, however precious this may have been in earlier periods of human history. For to stem the tragedies of racialism or mass political movements which are careless of human suffering we may need a mutation of the traditional concept of holiness. Love is always mysterious in its workings, and there is no doubt that any predictions about the course it will take are bound to be falsified by events. There is no doubt also that much that we have learned to expect from love – the ordinariness, the familiarity, the simplicity, the de-egocentricising power of it, will remain constant. But nevertheless perhaps what will happen will be a moving away from the lovely and haunting vision of perfection in a tiny handful of men and women to a new understanding of how the seeds of wholeness might be coaxed to grow amongst a much wider section of the population. Only so can the great avalanches of hatred, fear and unreality be stopped, as men learn to fight the battle of the devil within instead of attacking him in their religious or political opponent, their unrighteous or coloured neighbour, or members of their own family.

One might perhaps claim that there always has been a wealth of goodness amongst ordinary, unmiraculous people – a long and glorious line of faithful lovers, faithful parents, faithful children, faithful friends, faithful neighbours, faithful citizens. Their deeds have not often come to light, but we have all seen them and experienced them, and owe whatever capacity we have for love to such prosaic goodness. It is often only possible to assess its glory and healing power by looking at its tragic opposite – the surrender to evil of many who from babyhood have been hurt, betrayed and deserted.

Perhaps it is only now when we see traditional values breaking up, and we know more of the psychological damage inflicted by lack of love in early childhood that we can look back and question a little the assumptions about holiness which Christians have tended to make. It is striking how few of the Church's saints have been married, and I notice that the examples of holiness in our time I have used earlier in this chapter all have a clerical flavour. Somehow we have conditioned ourselves to look for holiness among those who have made a certain sort of explicit commitment rather than among those who are committed just by being men and women, husbands or wives, fathers or mothers. What we have looked for we have tended to find.

To heal the terrible wounds of mankind we need to value this most ordinary commitment of just being a human being and seek to add nothing more dramatic to it. We need to love Edward and Lavinia's courage as well as Celia's, as they struggle with the crucifixion of their alienation and despair. We need to recognise and applaud in one another the drive towards wholeness — towards self-understanding and the pain and victory it brings. Edward and Lavinia, just as much as Celia, have to make a bewildering and lonely journey "the process by which the human is transhumanised". They too will pass "between the scolding hills, the valley of derision", as anyone who tries to love and to care in our society is bound to do. They will have to battle with their ambition and materialism, with their fears that everything, including love, may be meaningless, with their aversion to suffering, to darkness, to the pressure of the numinous. That they should make the attempt is our only hope.

C

Holiness in
The Anglican Tradition

by

A. M. ALLCHIN

A. M. Allchin, M.A., B.Litt., was born in London in 1930. He was educated at Westminster School, Christ Church, Oxford and Cuddesdon College, Oxford. Ordained deacon and priest, he was a curate at St. Mary Abbots, Kensington, from 1956 to 1960 and Librarian Pusey House, Oxford, from 1960 to 1969. He is now Warden of the Community of the Sisters of the Love of God, Fairacres, Oxford. His books include *The Silent Rebellion, The Spirit of the Word, A Rapture of Praise* (with Professor H. A. Hodges), and *The Rediscovery of Newman* (with John Coulson). He is also a member of the Archbishop's Commission on Doctrine and of the Commission on Inter-communion.

HOLINESS is about a festival of joy, a dinner party to which all the most unlikely people are invited. For holiness is about God giving his life and love to men, and men giving their life and love to one another in a movement of joy which overflows in thankfulness to God the giver. The Gospels are full of stories about meals taken together, about great ceremonial feasts, about family celebrations with music and dancing, when someone who has been missing suddenly turns up, about breakfast by the lake-side in the summer dawn, with fish and bread cooking on the stones. The holiness of God is always what we least expected. It works itself out in flesh and blood.

We did not expect to see the flesh and blood of a man nailed to a cross, as the centre of the way that leads to this celebration of joy, as the heart of the truth about this world which was made good, as the source of the life which goes beyond death. But that is how it is. For joy cannot be known in this world without suffering, and suffering in this world can be the way that leads to joy. Man is, as we know him, alienated from God, alienated from his own true self. The common banquet in which all are called to share is divided and split into hostile, greedy, malevolent factions. Man is divided against himself and against God. He is cut off from the deepest sources of life and truth. It is God himself who re-opens the way to the restoration and renewal of the fullness of man's being. It is God himself who in Jesus of Nazareth unlooses the springs and frees the creative waters of man's spirit with the gift of his free Spirit. It is he who by going down into death overcomes death and opens the land of life to all who will come in.

God does this in man. For Jesus is no less truly man than he is truly God. In him mankind is restored to that union and communion for which we were made; in him the image and likeness of the Father's love is fully revealed. In the power of the Holy Spirit, God himself at work in the hearts and minds and hands of men, all men can find themselves at one in Jesus Christ, all men again can find themselves one family in God our Father. From the north and the south, from the east and the west all the scattered families of man can come and sit down at the royal festival of God's humanity. For the Spirit of God whose coming the Lord prepared is the Spirit of sonship and of freedom, the Spirit in whom man's life is restored to its true dimensions of eternity and joy.

The gift of holiness

All this is a gift, a constantly renewed gift. To be a human being is to receive and to give. We receive our life as a gift from others, and we in return are enabled to give life to others. We receive and give food and clothing, care and skills, love and insight. And all this mutual giving and receiving itself flows out of the infinite giving of God, our receiving from him and our being enabled even to give back to him praise and worship, love and gratefulness. These are the saints, who receive their life as a free gift from God, a gift at every moment full of the fearful richness of the giver, and who are enabled to give back beauty, love and life itself to the one from whom beauty, love and life have come. The saints are life-givers to their fellow-men, because they themselves have received life from the Lord and giver of life who dwells within them.

All men are called to be saints, called to give and to receive life, to accept their life as a gift from God and to offer it back to him in thankfulness and praise. All those who are Christ's explicitly do these things in every act of faith in God in Christ, and specifically in those strangely simple acts of Baptism and Eucharist, in which we receive God's life as a gift and are enabled by the Spirit to offer our lives in return in adoration to him. All men are called to give life to their neighbours and to receive life at their hands, parents and children in one way, friends and fellow workers in another, husbands and wives in another. All those who are Christ's find the meaning and the way of this exchange of life and love, in the pattern of his self-giving who by his death gave life to the world.

Thus those who are called saints are only those who have realised in a full and splendid way the vocation that is common to all, common to all Christians, common to all men. In them we recognise what we are called to be, in them we see the beginnings of the glory of the humanity which God has made and loved. That glory is as unexpected as the glory which is revealed in and through the Cross. The fullest pattern of humanity which we have in the Gospels and in those who live by the Gospels, is not a pattern of completion in this world, of self-satisfaction and integration in this world.

Certainly the ideal of a balanced and integrated personality, which is the aim of much contemporary living, is not alien to the Christian notion of sanctity. Balance, integration and maturity, these are good things and things to be sought. But in a world so evidently wounded as our own any self-enclosed integration would be intolerable. We must be prepared to be open to the world and open, too, to the demands of God. Our ideal of human integration must be set within a larger context. Sanctity is to be seen in that wholeness which is yet an open, vulnerable wholeness, the pattern of fully human living. It is a pattern of joy through sorrow, of making through breaking. In the light which breaks into this world of sin and death, of space and time, in the lives of the saints it becomes clear that here we have no abiding city, and that we ourselves and all things with us are hungry and thirsty, waiting on tip toe to receive a gift which as yet we only glimpse. As he faced death in the Roman arena, Ignatius of Antioch said, "Now I begin to be a disciple . . . Suffer me to receive the pure light. When I come thither, then I shall be a man. Permit me to be an imitator of the passion of my God." A great Moslem man of prayer declared, "Those whose wound is named Jesus can never be cured." In the saints God deepens that wound in our wounded world so that his merciful and healing grace may flow into it to prepare its final transformation and resurrection.

Saints and their diversity

Man was made by God to find this unbelievable fulfilment in union with him. He was made in God's image and likeness, in order that he might share in the divine nature and be partaker of God's holiness. There is in the heart and mind of every man an infinite capacity for sorrow and joy, for understanding and love, a capacity which seldom seems to be fully realised. But when it is realised, when we can see it in flesh and blood, then we know it, and recognise it as being the real thing. For what is true of each human being is true of all. All men are made as one man. All are members one of another and share a common nature. We are all one flesh. Each unique and unrepeatable human person can find life only as he enters into a free and mutual relationship with all his fellow human beings, can sit down with them at the table of mankind, and share in the common feast which Love provides, in which he gives us himself. In finding one another in the midst of life, we also find God. And in finding God, we discover who we truly are, what is the depth and glory of our human existence, and what is the true meaning of love as between persons.

The very possibility therefore of the recognition of "Saints" by the

Church, that is to say their public proclamation and commemoration, depends on this inner likeness, this hidden affinity between them and the whole Christian people, indeed between them and the whole human race. It is because we recognise in them the growth of the life which is shared between us, that we are able with gratefulness to celebrate what God has done in them. The process of recognition, or "canonisation" as it is called, when it is properly understood, does not involve any separation of the saints from us their fellow men. Rather the reverse is true; they are now recognised as fully human and accessible. For since their life is now indeed hid with Christ in God, they are intimately and mysteriously present with us.

The process of canonisation, this public recognition of what God has done through the life of a particular member of the Christian family, is conducted in different ways in different parts of the Church of God. The Roman Catholic Church, for instance, has very full and detailed ways of testing and proving the assertion of an individual's sanctity. The various Eastern Orthodox Churches generally proceed in a simpler way in the official proclamation of their more recent saints as, for instance, in the canonisation of St. Nektarios of Aegina (1846-1920) in Greece, or in the canonisation of a group of Romanian saints in 1955. But even so this is not done without careful investigation, and in pre-revolutionary Russia there could be a very full enquiry, as in the case of St. Seraphim of Sarov, canonised in 1903. In the Anglican Communion, the need for a fuller recognition and commemoration of the saints whom God has given to the Church has been increasingly felt in the present century, and various proposals have been made for the inclusion of more recent names in the Church's Calendar.[1]

But the reasons for which this recognition is accorded seem themselves to have varied to some extent in the course of the Church's history. The Church has always, it is true, been concerned to acclaim what God has done in and through a particular person, to recognise in their life and death a notable sign from God. In the first centuries of our history, when it was popular acclaim alone which made the recognition, it was the martyrs who had given their life for Christ who were seen as the models of Christian faith and life for all. In the period following the peace of the Church, we can see that saints were often recognised not only or perhaps primarily on account of the faultlessness of their lives,

---

[1] See especially, *The Commemoration of Saints and Heroes in the Faith*, a report prepared for the Lambeth Conference of 1958. S.P.C.K. The most striking instance in modern Anglican practice of official commemmoration and veneration of a saint is that of Bernard Mizeki. See *Mashonaland Martyr, Bernard Mizeki and the Pioneer Church*, by Jean Farrant, 1966.

but because of the role which God had given them to play in the history of his people. The Emperor Constantine of Byzantium was called "equal to the apostles" not on account of his personal character but because of what he stood for in the conversion of the Empire. Jerome was recognised as a Doctor of the Church, despite, one might think, certain of his traits of temperament, because of what he had been given to do in the pentecostal work of translating the Scriptures.

In more recent centuries, in all the Churches, there has been a tendency to think of holiness almost exclusively in personal and inward terms, so that it has been much easier for a nun to be canonised than a great theologian, and much easier for a theologian than a great statesman. But this surely is to value the integrity and wholeness of a life given to God in prayer and silence, at the expense of the different kind of integrity and wholeness which is to be found in one who has sought to serve God through all the vicissitudes of a long life of intellectual effort or political combat, lived in the midst of the affairs of the world. It is to restrict the meaning of holiness too narrowly to one type of holiness. It involves no denial of the transparent glory of a St. Thérèse of Lisieux, to wish that it might be easier to envisage the recognition of the different glory of a John Henry Newman, or of even a William Gladstone. If in the latter part of this chapter some names are mentioned which may seem surprising in an account of English holiness, this is the reason why. They are all men in whom God's will was manifestly done, in one way or another; in some cases men, who despite their own failures and weaknesses, were signs from God for a whole society or a whole generation. In them we see pre-eminent traces of that life of holiness which is given to all Christians, even if it was not in every way fully developed in them.

The basic pattern of holiness, of life in Christ, is common to all Christians. It is the pattern of Christ's own life, a pattern of life through death, of self-giving love. This life of God in the life of man does not destroy all the diversity and multiplicity of the world which is itself the work of God. It breaks down the barriers and separations between men, it reveals to them the reality and meaning of their common nature; but it in no way makes for uniformity or sameness. There is a strong family likeness among the saints but at the same time each is a unique and unrepeatable person. To find ourselves in God is to find our true selves, to become the person we were made to be, not to be conformed to some external pattern or example. All the natural endowments of a person, his family background, his cultural and social gifts, his intellectual and human formation, his national characteristics, all these things are not destroyed in man's growth towards maturity in God. They are taken and transformed. The world of time and space cannot encompass God's Kingdom of eternity, but it is taken up into it, in the resurrection of the body. Thus within the whole realm of Christian holiness, we may properly discern a Russian, an Italian, an English type of sanctity; and knowing that these national characteristics are of only secondary importance, can yet rejoice to see how in the Kingdom of God nothing that is good is lost.

There is also within Christendom a diversity which comes from the different ways of understanding the fullness of Christian faith and life which have developed in the different portions of the Christian family. The grace of God mediated through the sacraments, the reading of the Bible, the practice of prayer and the whole tradition of Christian love in action, constantly breaks through and transfigures even very partial and one-sided presentations of the Christian message. Nonetheless it is true that what people are taught to expect from God does, in some measure, condition their ability to receive what God has to give.

Many parts of Reformation Christendom, not all and certainly not authentic Methodism, have been much less hopeful about the extent to which man might advance into the fulness of the divine life even in this world, than Catholicism and Orthodoxy have been. If the history of Protestantism has not been marked by the appearance of so many outstanding examples of Christian holiness, perhaps this fact may account for it. It seems as if, in the sixteenth century, the reformers were forced to take a new and deeper look at the reality of sin in the life of the Church and in the life of the believer. They were in reaction against the naïve and perhaps sub-Christian optimism of the Middle Ages, in reaction against an admiration for holiness which had been dazzled by its peripheral and secondary manifestations, the miraculous and extra-ordinary, and had tended to lose sight of its hidden and infinitely precious core, love, joy and peace. The reformers therefore stressed the fact that in this life man always stands in need of the mercy of God, and they looked with great reserve on stories of those who had been filled with superhuman power. There was in this reaction something good and true. Man does always stand in need of God's forgiveness; the true glory of holiness is revealed not in exterior and surprising events and sayings, but in an inner transformation of life and understanding, something which the great writers of the saints' lives had always stressed, even in the Middle Ages. At the same time, with their repudiation of monasticism, and their insistence on the fact that every believer is responsible before God, the reformers gave a new sense of the meaning of holiness for the Christian living and working in the world.

If Protestantism has not in general looked for heroic sanctity of the type of a St. Francis or a St. Teresa, it has looked for and received from God a quality of simple hidden Christian life in family and home, in trade and agriculture which is one of the glories of the whole of Christendom. All this is positive. But on the other side it must be said that in many parts of Protestantism there has been a constant tendency, helped on by certain unhappy ways of formulating belief, to cease to look for any radiant transformation in the life of man in this world. It has been, and it is, possible to take the formula that man in Christ is before God always *simul justus et peccator*, one who in Christ is righteous and yet in himself always in need of the divine pity, to mean that God simply accepts us as we are, and leaves us as we are, that Christ's righteousness is imputed to us, but not imparted. This may not be the true interpretation of the formula. It is unfortunately one which has at times prevailed. It is this tendency within Protestantism which so often has turned the life of the Protestant Churches in the English-speaking world into a simple mirror image of the life of respectable middle-class society. In answer to this the certainty of both Catholicism and Orthodoxy that at least in some of his servants God works a glorious transfiguration even now speaks with something of the boldness of the New Testament itself.

The historic pattern of Anglican holiness

One of the great problems about speaking of the Anglican tradition of holiness is that it is a tradition marked, to a certain extent, both by national and by theological considerations. On the one side it is not like, let us say, the Russian tradition of holiness, simply the national expression of a single, unified Christian life. The Anglican tradition of holiness has been strongly marked in its later centuries by the events of the reformation. On the other hand because Anglicans, particularly those who live in the British Isles, have on the whole had a stronger sense of the continuity and identity of their Church through the reformation events than has been the case with most Protestants, and because again Anglicanism has not made anything like such a clearly-defined and systematic statement of the Christian faith as have Lutheranism and

Calvinism, it is equally impossible to regard it simply as one of the traditions of spiritual life and understanding derived directly from the reformation. What we shall find is a national tradition of holiness, in which in its later stages certain features become particularly marked, on account both of the influence of theological factors, and of a period of comparative isolation from the greater part of the Christian tradition.

When we speak of the national tradition which is behind Anglicanism, we are at once confronted with a further problem. The Christian faith was established in the British Isles before the arrival of the people whose language has come to be English. The Church of the English people received its hierarchy from the mission of Pope Gregory in 597, when St. Augustine set up his diocese in Canterbury, but its life has been deeply influenced by the witness and the sanctity of the Church already founded in these islands in the centuries before the Anglo-Saxon invasions. Particularly in the North and West of England the influence of Celtic saints and Celtic holy places, outstanding among them Glastonbury and Lindisfarne, has been and remains considerable.

The whole conversion of the North of England came originally from Ireland, through Iona, where Columba had established his community. From Iona, Aidan came to Lindisfarne and preached the Gospel throughout Northumbria. Cuthbert (d. 687) carried on his mission. The names and memories of these men live on in the places where they lived and worked, particularly perhaps at Durham where Cuthbert lies buried in the great Cathedral church. They speak of a meeting and blending of Celt and Anglo-Saxon in the common faith of Christ, a meeting which produced much that is most precious in the first centuries of the Christianity of our lands; the love of learning, the fervent devotion to Christ, the love of all creation, especially of the animals both those who roam at large and those who share man's dwelling and his labours. The provinces of the Anglican Communion in the three Celtic nations of the British Isles, Ireland, Scotland and Wales, are now only minority Churches, but the contribution of these people and of their ancient Christian tradition to the Church of the English has always been of great importance.

But in the development of Anglicanism it is necessarily of the Church of England that we have to think first and, looking back through the fourteen centuries of the history of that Church, we must try to discern certain common characteristics which mark it over that long period of time. Is it possible to find traits of character which remain constant in Anglo-Saxon England, in the centuries of the high Middle Ages and the Renaissance, in the period of the Reformation and down to our day? We shall suggest, tentatively, that it is.

If we look at two of the greatest figures of the Anglo-Saxon Church we can already see something of the particular pattern of English sanctity. In the Venerable Bede (672-735) whose body also rests at Durham we have the foundation of the English pattern of Christian scholarship. We have a man of profound scriptural and historical learning, not a philosophical or speculative intellect. We have a historian working at a time of the greatest difficulty and showing at such a moment in history truly admirable qualities of judgement and balance. We have a man whose intellectual genius was all at the service of the Church's faith and life. Bede has been recognised throughout the history of the English Church not as one of the most popular of English saints but as one who in a certain way typified virtues which his fellow-countrymen have come especially to prize.

When we turn from scholarship to national life, in King Alfred (849-899) we have certainly one of the greatest figures in the whole of English history. It is a strange and somewhat disquieting fact about the Church of his own and subsequent centuries, that he was not officially remembered among the saints of Anglo-Saxon England. Only in our own century was his name introduced into the Calendar of the Church of England, and surely it was done with justice. Here again we find the passion of balance and judgement which we noticed in Bede, but this time exercised in the realm of political and civil authority. We have too a concern for learning and for the well-being of the Church, which is especially remarkable in relation to the age in which he lived. And, as in Bede, we find a close connection with and a discerning appreciation of the faith of the non-English peoples of these islands. In Alfred's close association with his biographer Asser, Bishop of St. David's, one finds an awareness of the diversity of national life in Britain which has not always been a characteristic of the English. But already in these two great figures of the Anglo-Saxon centuries, we see some of the particular qualities which become a constant feature of English sanctity.

When we move into the centuries after the Norman Conquest, in which our country was drawn into closer association with Europe, this same spirit of balance and wisdom is not lost. One of the greatest and most attractive of all English saints is St. Aelred of Rievaulx (1109-1167) one who is worthy to stand with St. Bernard and William of St. Thierry as among the leaders of the Cistercian movement, that movement to which Englishmen, one might also mention St. Stephen Harding and Isaac of Stella, were to contribute so much.

In St. Aelred there is a combination of qualities which, for all his close connection with the continent, mark the twelfth-century Abbot as distinctively English. There is the love for history, which we have already noticed in Bede, for the history of his own nation and his own birth-place, Hexham, where his father had been the hereditary priest. There is the love for Scripture, and the same disinclination for speculative and systematic theology. There is the wonderful sense of pastoral responsibility, which shines out in many of his writings, and which made the Abbey of Rievaulx a place where both strong and weak could find life under his gentle but discerning guidance. Above all there is the conviction which his whole life and teaching expresses, that grace does not overthrow nature, but fulfils and perfects it. In what other writer of the Middle Ages is there so fine and joyful a discussion of the nature of human friendship, and of the way in which human love can be transformed and lifted up into the divine love? If in an age of violent change like our own we wish to rediscover in our national history figures who can be of healing significance for our own generation, there are few to whom we could more confidently turn than Aelred.[1]

In the history of the English language, no less than in the history of English spirituality, the fourteenth century has a special place. It is a time of a sudden flowering which saw three of the first great poets of our modern language at work, Chaucer, Langland and the author of *Sir Gawayne and the Green Knight,* three writers amazingly distinct from one another, yet all in their different ways conveying a richly Christian vision of human life and society. It was also the time of the greatest single school of English mystical and spiritual writing yet to have been given to us; the time of *The Cloud of Unknowing* and Walter Hilton, of Richard Rolle and Julian of Norwich. It is perhaps again a sign of the malaise of later mediaeval Christendom that none of these writers was ever formally recognised among the saints of the Church. Indeed for centuries after the reformation they fell into almost complete oblivion. Only within the last fifty years has their influence and attractiveness become widely known and felt. Virginia Woolf, for instance, in the years after the first world war, writing a perceptive essay on English women writers could still be entirely ignorant of the existence of Lady Julian. Now the recluse of Norwich begins to be acknowledged as a

---

[1] A very fine picture of Aelred can be found in *Aelred of Rievaulx, a Study* by Aelred Squire o.p., S.P.C.K. 1969.

writer whose importance is not for England alone, but for all of Christendom, one who is not only a devotional but a theological teacher of the Church.

> "There can be no doubt," writes Thomas Merton, "that Lady Julian is the greatest of the English mystics. Not only that, but she is one of the greatest English theologians, in the ancient sense of the word. As Evagrius Ponticus said in the fourth century, 'He who really prays is a theologian, and he who is a theologian really prays.' By prayer, of course, this Desert Father meant the 'theologia', which was at once the contemplation and experience of the deepest revealed mysteries, the mystical knowledge of the Holy Trinity. Actually in Julian of Norwich we find an admirable synthesis of mystical experience and theological reflection, ranging from 'bodily visions' of the Passion of Christ, to 'intellectual visions' of the Trinity, and from reflections on the creation and providence to intuitions penetrating the inmost secret of redemption and the divine mercy."[1]

In nothing is the wisdom and insight of Lady Julian more evidently seen than in the way in which she holds together the Church's faith in divine judgement, with her own assurance that "all shall be well". The repeated word of the Lord regarding the restoration of all things is not given to one who had ignored the realities of sin and suffering and death, but rather to one who had plumbed them as deeply as it is given to the human heart and mind to do. This is what gives to her optimism a quality utterly different from the optimism which simply speaks of the "best of all possible worlds". As Father Merton writes in another place, "She must indeed believe and accept the fact that there is a hell, yet at the same time, impossibly one would think, she believes even more firmly that 'the word of Christ shall be saved in all things' and 'all manner of things shall be well.' This is, for her, the heart of theology, not solving the contradiction, but remaining in the midst of it, in peace, knowing that it is fully solved, but that the solution is secret, and will never be guessed until it is revealed."[2]

It is not for nothing that the fourteenth century saw this flowering both of English literature and spirituality, and that those great and profound works of mystical theology, *The Revelations of Divine Love*, and

---

[1] Thomas Merton, *Mystics and Zen Masters*. p. 2. New York: Farrar, Strauss and Giroux, dist. Burns, Oates.

[2] Thomas Merton, *Conjectures of a Guilty Bystander*. p. 192. Burns, Oates.

The Cloud of Unknowing should have been written in the English language, one of them by a laywoman or nun. The history of English sanctity is from the beginning intertwined with the history of the language. We may think of Alfred's care to have translations made from the Latin, or of Aelred on his death-bed praying for the end to hasten "for Crist luve". because the word "Christ" has a simpler and sweeter sound in the English tongue. It seems as though at the end of the fourteenth century, before the turmoils and schisms which were to follow a little over a hundred years later, something was being prepared for an alliance between poetic and mystical insight, between the love of letters and the desire for God which was to survive all the subsequent vicissitudes, and was to give to the English people the richest heritage of Christian and theological poetry of any European nation.[1] Furthermore and more profoundly, it was not for nothing that both the Lady Julian and the unknown author of *The Cloud*, should have taken up in their writings some of the deepest themes of the Eastern Orthodox tradition, for here again is a quality which becomes plainly evident in later Anglicanism, this profound if sometimes hidden affinity with Eastern Orthodoxy.

It is difficult to write of the sixteenth century in connection with sanctity. Not that saints are lacking in that troubled, creative and yet disastrous epoch. On both sides men and women went to atrocious deaths in order to witness to the utmost to the truth of Christ as they understood it. In our own times surely it is for Anglicans to commemorate those for whose deaths our fathers in the faith were responsible, Edmund Campion, Margaret Clitheroe and a host of other martyrs, and for Roman Catholics to remember the figures of Latimer, Ridley and Cranmer with all their companions, whose martyrdoms burnt themselves deeply into the memory of the English people. Meanwhile there is one saint who suffered in this time, who already acts as a reconciling figure, and already attracts the veneration of Anglicans and Roman Catholics alike, St. Thomas More (1478-1535). Here rather than in the king whom he served is the true successor of Alfred, as a type of the Christian statesman. To the qualities which we have already noticed as typical of English sanctity, all of which are to be observed in More, we may add his sense of humour.

After the sixteenth century, in speaking of the tradition of Anglican sanctity we no longer speak of the whole Christian tradition of the

[1] On this theme see R. W. Chambers' *On the Continuity of English Prose from Alfred to More and his School*. O.U.P., 1932.

English people. On both sides of the Church of England traditions emerge which have their rightful place within the history of God's dealings with our people but which no longer form part of the national Church. In this sense the Anglican tradition becomes a more limited thing. Furthermore qualities of moderation, discretion, balance and humanness which we have already discerned became more noticeable and noticeable perhaps in a more limiting way. Christian sanctity has in it an element of the absurd, the paradoxical, the extreme; but in seventeenth-century England for instance one would be more likely to find these qualities among the early Quakers or in the heroic courage of the recusant clergy than among the members of the Church established. Furthermore the Church of England was deeply influenced by the general reformation distrust for too easy an acceptance of the miraculous, and also by the new emphasis on the vocation of the married Christian in the world. The monastic orders disappeared, though we may see some echo of their ideal in the life at Little Gidding, and in the example of such great unmarried Bishops as Lancelot Andrewes and Thomas Ken. Nonetheless the usual pattern of Anglican holiness becomes that of the married state, whether in the home of priest or layman.

If the seventeenth century was like the sixteenth, a time of violent controversy and religious strife, yet it has also strange affinities with the fourteenth. In the theology of Richard Hooker (1554-1600) a masterpiece of English writing, no less than of theological analysis, in the poetry of George Herbert, Henry Vaughan and Thomas Traherne, in the preaching of Lancelot Andrewes and Jeremy Taylor, we have a presentation of the Christian mystery, a vision of the nature of the faith and Gospel, which is certainly much richer and more complex in its articulation than that of the earlier time, even if it lacks some elements of its all-inclusive wholeness. The Anglicans of this century could not avoid being caught up in the polemics of their age, but already they had caught the vision of a Catholicism which would be larger than that of Rome, which would reconcile East and West, and would incorporate all that was valid in the witness of the reformers. No moment in the century more typically represents the spirit of Anglican holiness than the story of Little Gidding where the family of the Ferrars together set themselves to live a Christian community and family life with a seriousness and joy which sound the authentic note of Christian sanctity. Here again in the whole history of this experiment there is a sanctified naturalness, a mingling of the homely with the holy, which might seem

D

almost too comfortable were it not matched with the deeply supernatural character of Nicholas Ferrar himself (1592-1637), the leader of
the enterprise. Many drew new hope and inspiration for their own life in
Christ from the community at Little Gidding, not least George Herbert,
and King Charles I, who redeemed his weaknesses in the manner of his
death. In our own time its example has come to life again in the work of
T. S. Eliot. In one of the greatest of English theological poems[1], there
are lines which can tell us much about the nature of holy places and the
tradition of the saints.

> "If you came this way,
> Taking any route, starting from anywhere,
> At any time or at any season,
> It would always be the same: you would have to put off
> Sense and notion. You are not here to verify,
> Instruct yourself, or inform curiosity
> Or carry report. You are here to kneel
> Where prayer has been valid. And prayer is more
> Than an order of words, the conscious occupation
> Of the praying mind, or the sound of the voice praying.
> And what the dead had no speech for, when living,
> They can tell you, being dead: the communication
> Of the dead is tongued with fire beyond the language of the living.
> Here the intersection of the timeless moment
> Is England and nowhere. Never and always."

The strident and violent religious polemics of the seventeenth
century subsided into the superficial calm of the eighteenth. Beneath
the calm, and on the edges of the polite society of the enlightenment,
the vision of God remained. It burst open in the praise of a poet who
became mad, Christopher Smart; it nourished the life of a mystic who
withdrew into obscurity, William Law; it achieved magnificent expression in the sermons and hymns of the brothers Wesley who defied all the
conventions of their time in order to bring the news of God's revelation
in Christ to the most illiterate of their fellow-men. In any record of
Anglican sanctity the names and the work of John and Charles Wesley
must stand high. At the same time they must provide a question mark.
For though both of them died as they had lived as priests of the Church
of England, the magnificent theological and spiritual vision which they
had proclaimed could not be contained within the bounds of the

1 "Little Gidding" by T. S. Eliot. The last of *Four Quartets*. Faber and Faber, 1944.

established Church. Only in a reconciliation of Anglican and Methodist traditions shall we begin to understand more fully all that God is willing to teach us through them.

But there is one figure who stands at the centre of the eighteenth century scene, one whose character is intimately known to us, whose imperfections are plain, whose character yet deserves to be pondered very deeply in this context of the witness of a Christian life, and that is Samuel Johnson (1709-1784). In defiance of all the fashions of his age, in defiance of his own deep despairs and anxieties, Johnson retained his faith in the Triune God of the Catholic tradition. In his own person he seems to bear up the literary and social world of eighteenth-century London, obstinately maintaining his practice of prayer and fasting, his participation in the Sacraments, not being ashamed to kneel beside the death-bed of the old maid-servant who had looked after him in child-hood. The pattern of holiness varies greatly from century to century, from one man to another. Is it perverse to see elements of it in the great-ness of Samuel Johnson?

Evangelical and Catholic holiness

Out of the Evangelical revival in which the Wesleys had played such a conspicuous part, many consequences flowed for the future of English Christianity, and indeed of the whole Christian world. Not least among them was a new awareness of the incompatibility of the institution of slavery with the Christian understanding of man. This understanding incarnated itself in the person of a single man, who devoted his whole life to the abolition of the slave-trade, and to the diffusion of "practical Christianity". William Wilberforce (1759-1833) renounced the ordi-nary rewards of the political career which could certainly have been his in order to give himself to this one thing. Once again we have the example of the Christian layman, of the one who lives the message which he preaches.

But the campaign for the abolition of the slave-trade did not exhaust the Evangelicals' concern for the world beyond the confines of the old European Christendom. A new missionary fervour stirred the Church of England in the first years of the nineteenth century, and in Henry Martyn (1781-1812), produced one of the great creative figures of Anglican Evangelicalism. After a brilliant career at Cambridge, Martyn abandoned the prospects of academic preferment and in 1805 at the call of God set sail for India where he devoted his great intellectual and linguistic gifts to translating the New Testament and the preaching of the Gospel. He died in Persia in 1812, having burnt himself out in seven years of intense activity. One of his friends in India, writing home to report the decline of his strength in these last years, adds in a memorable phrase, "In all other respects he is exactly the same as he was; he shines in all the dignity of love; and he seems to carry about him such a heavenly majesty, as impresses the mind beyond description." The example of such a life, given in such an unprecedented way to the service of the Gospel, gave a pattern which many later nineteenth-century missionaries sought to emulate.[1]

In England itself, the movement did much to raise the whole conception of the role of the ministry of the Church. Here the man who had been Henry Martyn's vicar during his brief curacy in Cambridge, Charles Simeon (1759-1836) was of outstanding importance. For over fifty years he ministered in Holy Trinity, Cambridge, and influenced generations of undergraduates. Through the eccentricities of his style and manner, the grace of God shone out, a challenge to the complacency of his contemporaries. Simeon had been converted in his own student days at King's College in the course of Holy Week, 1779. It was an experience which was sealed and crowned at the Holy Communion on Easter Sunday. Looking back much later over the passage of his life, he could say, "There are but two objects that I have ever desired for these forty years to behold; the one is my own vileness; and the other is the glory of God in the face of Jesus Christ; and I have always thought that they should be viewed together; just as Aaron confessed all the sins of all Israel whilst he put them on the head of the scapegoat. The disease did not keep him from applying the remedy, nor did the remedy keep him from feeling the disease. By this I seek to be, not only *humbled* and *thankful*, but *humbled* in *thankfulness* before my God and Saviour continually. This is the religion which pervades the whole Liturgy, and particularly the Communion Service, and this makes the Liturgy inexpressibly sweet to me."[2] These remarkable words show how, contrary to common belief, the life of such a man could be shaped not only by the personal prayer of forgiveness (what in Orthodoxy would be "the Jesus prayer") but also by the spirit of the Eucharist.

In its later manifestations the Evangelical style of Christian life has left an uncertain memory, and has been associated with an idea of narrowness and rigidity which excluded much that is human from the

---

[1] See: C. E. Padwick, *Henry Martyn, Confessor of the Faith.* Inter-Varsity Press, 1953.
[2] M. A. C. Warren, *Strange Victory.* Canterbury Press, 1946.

grace of Christ. It is good to read the biographies of the early Evangelicals like William Wilberforce and Henry Thornton, Henry Martyn and Charles Simeon to find how much fuller their living of the Christian life was, than their theology would sometimes lead us to suspect. In its movement towards God, and in its movement towards man, made in God's image and redeemed in Christ, it had a vigour and a fullness which is unmistakable.

But it was above all in the men who were typical of the movement which began in the nineteenth century in Oxford, that the Anglican type of holiness received its most splendid illustrations. From many it is difficult to know whom to choose. Three names may be taken as representative, a priest, a bishop and a layman.

John Keble (1792-1866) was in many ways the fountain head of the whole Oxford Movement. Others were more brilliant and forceful preachers and writers than he, others more massive scholars, more determined propagandists. But no one so typified as he did that combination of a longing for holiness, with a realisation of the value of this life and its goodness, which was characteristic of the Oxford Movement. No one too typified more than Keble, that love of hiddenness, that hatred of display which again was typical of all the men who followed his example. Pusey who had known him intimately for many years records, "Above all he lived. The passion of his Lord whom he loved, was his book, his life. He lived, because Christ lived in him. He was all prayer at all times, but only those who observed him closely could perceive it; had he known it was perceived he would have hid it. His humbling humility was even surprising, startling. The strong light of the sun penetrating into our dwellings shows us the grains of dust not seen before. It is the character of saints to believe themselves least of all. He talked no controversy, but he lived; and doubting minds were impressed and said 'God is in us of a truth.'"

But still more than in John Keble, the beauty of holiness was revealed in Edward King, Bishop of Lincoln (1829-1910) a man who has been more nearly officially canonised by our Church than any other of its more recent members. His contemporaries are unanimous in their testimony to him. "It was light that he carried with him – light that shone through him – light that flowed from him. The room was lit into which he entered. It was as if we had fallen under a streak of sunlight, that flickered and danced and laughed, and turned all to colour and to gold."[1]

[1] Owen Chadwick, *The Founding of Cuddesdon*; see the entire chapter on Edward King.

In Owen Chadwick's masterly character sketch of King as he was in his middle years as Principal of Cuddesdon, we can see as it were a summing-up of all that is best in the post-Reformation Anglican tradition of holiness, and something that is characteristic of that tradition in its totality.

"The first quality which men saw was his gentleness. . . . You cannot look at the Richmond portrait of King and miss the gentleness. But you can not suppose it to be the gentleness of weakness, the gentleness of insignificance. The gentleness was that of a controlled strength. Yet somehow the control was neither forced nor evident. There is a saintliness which seems to spring from vigorous self-discipline. King's character did not suggest to his men that kind of quality. About the self-discipline there could be no doubt. But what was evident was the humanity, the breadth, the naturalness. They found in him no tension, no pose, no tautness that he could not relax. He was one of those rare spirits in whom grace seems natural. 'Grace had so intimately mingled with his nature that it was all of one piece. Grace itself had become natural. Who was to say which was which? Was it all grace? Was it all nature? Was it not all both?' The Christian life, he made them feel, was supernatural, yes; other-worldly, yes; but not strange, or unnatural, or forced, or inhuman, or narrow. This was what man was born for. It was normality itself. It was balanced, sane, unwarped. It was man as he ought to be."

In the whole of his time as Principal of Cuddesdon, in training men for the priesthood, as in his work as Bishop of Lincoln, King "taught continuously the spiritual value of the Anglican 'You may', in contrast with the Roman 'You must'. He revelled in the blend of the appeal to authority and of the appeal to the free personal conscience. He was steeped in the typical traditions of our particular expression of Catholic Christianity." In his theological and spiritual teaching no less than in his constant and discerning pastoral care for those who were committed to his charge he always stressed the need to allow things to grow gradually. "He rarely set before his men words like *zeal* or *earnestness*. He was frightened of anything which suggested haste, rashness, over-pressure. The words which he set before them were words like *ripeness*, *maturity* . . . 'I do value so highly a natural growth in holiness, a humble, grateful acceptance of the circumstances God has provided for each of us, and I dread the unnatural, forced, cramped, ecclesiastical holiness,

which is so much more quickly produced, but is so human and poor.' "
He had great confidence in the power of grace to restore and renew the
nature of man, "The heart," he wrote, "is of such immense capacity, if
we will only give it up to God to discipline."

All this stress on naturalness and gradualness did not mean that
there was no element of challenge and demand in King's living of the
Christian life. But it did mean that he saw the glory of God which goes
beyond all that is of nature, revealed in and through the things of nature.
It was all of a piece with the theological vision of one who had meditated
on the mystery of the incarnation and the sacraments, under the guidance of theologians such as Richard Hooker and Lancelot Andrewes,
and who saw in Christ the fulfilment of all that is beautiful and true in
this world of space and time. One of Edward King's younger contemporaries, Fr. George Congreve, S.S.J.E. wrote, in words which might
be almost King's.

> "I quite believe in the Christian doctrine of self-denial, but I do
> not believe that it means, 'You must not love your garden or the
> old grey walls of Oxford, or the trees or the clouds, for fear you
> should love them instead of God.' I suspect that the true meaning
> of detachment and self-denial is rather, 'You must train yourself
> to pass from the love of these things in themselves, and in the
> comfort they are to you at this moment, to the love of them in God,
> i.e. to the love of what God means by them, His purpose in giving
> them to you for the moment, and that not always by refusing to
> look at them, but sometimes by "considering" them very gratefully
> and tenderly' . . . This is what St. Paul seems to mean by 'every
> creature of God is good . . . *if it be received with thanksgiving*,' with a
> love that is, which does not cleave to the creature, but goes on to
> God."[1]

The place of human relationship

Here is precisely the spirit in which seven centuries before Aelred had
written of human friendship. For if our love of the world in which we
are placed can be the means by which our hearts and minds rise to the
maker of the world in praise and gratitude, how much more is this true
of those whom God gives us to love as our friends. "And thus," wrote
the Cistercian Abbot, "beseeching Christ on behalf of one's friend, and
for the friend's sake desiring to be heard by Christ, the attention and

[1] W. H. Longridge [Ed.], *Spiritual Letters of Father Congreve.* pp. 122-3. Mowbrays.

affection are all directed to the friend; but suddenly and unawares love changes its object, and being so near touches the sweetness of Christ and begins to taste and feel how sweet he is, thus rising from that holy love which reaches the friend to that which reaches Christ." The writings of St. Aelred were not well known among the men of the Oxford Movement, but with their intense appreciation of the meaning of Christian friendship, they shared consciously or unconsciously in the same tradition of faith and life.

If the Church of England has come near to canonising Edward King, it never seems to have considered the possibility of canonising Mr. Gladstone (1809-1898). Yet in an earlier century of the Church there is no one perhaps who would have been more immediately recognised as one called out by God, to represent in his own person the Christian faith of an entire people. To recognise this quality in Mr. Gladstone does not mean to approve of everything in his character, still less to agree with every policy that he propounded. It means surely to recognise two things which mark him out as one of the great Christian statesmen of the modern world. First he symbolises, in the strongest possible sense, the combination of the Catholic tradition with the movement for change and development in the political and social realm. The whole tragedy of Christian Europe in the nineteenth century might be summed up in the divorce between the movements of political liberalism and radicalism, and the tradition of orthodox Christianity. Gladstone in his own person revealed that the divorce was not inevitable. But secondly, and still more revealing of the quality of the man, was his custom of walking out into the streets of London at night, and talking to prostitutes, inviting them back to his own house, so that he and his wife might try to help them and set them on a way of life more human and divine than that into which they had fallen. In itself it tells us much of Gladstone's character, that in all the violence of political controversy in which he was involved, and in all the love of scandal of nineteenth-century England, this practice was never made the basis of an attempt to blackmail him. But surely it tells us something more. For in the activity of the first minister of a great empire, going out into the streets of the city to find the most despised of his fellow human beings, we can hardly fail to see the image of the royal bounty of God which comes down into the deepest places of man's need. How in the Middle Ages men would have loved to celebrate the story of the king who at night went out in disguise amongst the lowest of his subjects seeking to rescue them from degradation and despair!

Signs of a new beginning

In this brief account of some of the great figures whom God has given to the Church of England, we may perhaps see something of the way in which God's action in redemption and sanctification is all of a piece with his action in creation. First we have noticed this link between English sanctity and English poetry, this quality of vision, which has given to many of our poets, to Herbert and Vaughan, to Christopher Smart and Blake, to Wordsworth and Browning, and in our own time to Edwin Muir and T. S. Eliot so central a place in our spiritual tradition. And surely it is in literature above all that God has given natural gifts to our people, and surely not without some purpose larger than our own, in so far as our language has become one of the international means of communication for an increasingly unified world. We have noticed next this chain of great administrators, from Alfred to More, to Wilberforce and Gladstone. At the moment when we finally relinquish our claims to imperial greatness, it is well to look over our past, both with repentance for all our terrible misuse of the power which we have been given over other nations, but also with gratitude for the fact that God has not left this element in our national history altogether unredeemed, but has given to us both in our legal and political history men and institutions whose significance goes beyond our own boundaries.

Since the time of the Oxford Movement, great and violent changes have taken place in our national and ecclesiastical life. We are only now at the beginning of what may be a long period of transformation. In terms of the Anglican tradition of spirituality and holiness, what has most impressed many Anglicans during this time is the limitation of our Anglican tradition, especially in its post-Reformation manifestation. There has been a longing for something more fully and inclusively catholic. Not that the gifts which God has given us in our own tradition are not true and precious. But they need to be complemented and corrected from other families within the Christian whole. Balance and discretion, judgement and modesty are great virtues. But so also are ecstasy and enthusiasm, and the whole-hearted acceptance of the absolutes of God's demand.

It is true that grace perfects and does not destroy our human nature; but the process of perfection may require a violence of breaking and remaking which at first sight appears anything but serene and calm. The fearful quality of the direct confrontation with the evil in man's heart which we see in such nineteenth-century saints as the Curé d'Ars in France, or St. Seraphim of Sarov in Russia, gives a strength and a toughness to the quality of their holiness which is desperately needed in the twentieth century. Looking back into the history of our Church, we cannot escape the fact that two of the most generous and noble men whom God has given in our life since the reformation, John Wesley and John Henry Newman, were unable to accept our Church's love for moderation and the judicious mean.

Nonetheless in this last century our tradition has begun to open itself out to the wider and deeper tradition of Christian sanctity. The revival of the monastic life has been one element in this development. In Fr. R. M. Benson, as in his spiritual father, E. B. Pusey, we have a man who knew in all its fierceness the inner conflict with evil, and who was not afraid to pay the cost. We have in our Church perhaps a privileged possibility of seeing the genuine reciprocity, the necessary mutual support which should exist between the Christian vocations to marriage and to single life. We have begun, though only begun, to recover that faith in the work of the Holy Spirit which will allow us again to commemorate the saints with joy and unselfconscious confidence, knowing that in the Holy Spirit they are not far from us, nor we from them. The holy places have again *begun* to be frequented, and we have begun, if yet only feebly, to realise that

"Wherever a saint has dwelt,
Wherever a martyr has given his blood for the blood of Christ,
There is holy ground, and the sanctity shall not depart from it.
From such ground springs that which forever renews the earth
Though it is forever denied."[1]

We have begun again to look for and to find in our own tradition the spiritual gifts of which St. Paul speaks in the apostolic Church, gifts of wisdom and discernment, of service and utterance, of healing and of tongues; and we have begun again to find in our own tradition that the signs which accompany sanctity are not always absent from among us, in such phenomena, insignificant perhaps in themselves, but full of meaning in relation to the loci in which they occur, of the stigmata and the transfiguration of the body. We look now for a fuller recovery of the great tradition, in which what God has given specifically to our people will find its place again in the harmony of the whole Christian family, and in which the ordinary believing people of England will find themselves to be in truth fellow-citizens with the saints and members of the household of God.

[1] *Murder in the Cathedral*, by T. S. Eliot. Faber and Faber, 1938.

Holiness
in
The Reformed Tradition

by

Geddes MacGregor

Geddes MacGregor, D.D., D.Phil., D. ès L., LL.B., F.R.S.L., was born in Scotland in 1909. He was a student at the University of Heidelberg, served in British Civil Defence in World War II and became a naturalised U.S. citizen in 1957. From 1949 to 1960 he was the first holder of the Rufus Jones Chair of Philosophy and Religion at Bryn Mawr College, U.S.A., and from 1960 to 1966 was Dean of the Graduate School of Religion. He now holds the title of Distinguished Professor of Philosophy in the University of Southern California. In the ministry of the Church of Scotland for over twenty-eight years, he has now become an Anglican priest and is Canon Theologian of St. Paul's Cathedral, Los Angeles. His books include *Introduction to Religious Philosophy, The Coming Reformation, The Hemlock and the Cross, God Beyond Doubt, A Literary History of the Bible* and *The Sense of Absence.*

The Reformation heritage

H OLINESS of life was, and always must be, of paramount importance to the heirs of the Reformation. The fruit of sanctification attests the goodness of the tree planted in God's garden. If such a tree does not bear this fruit it is plainly not of God's planting.

Sanctification is, no less than justification, a special emphasis of the Reformed tradition. Moreover, in the very sacramentalist view that the Reformers inherited from Calvin, whose vigorous opposition to the late mediaeval abuse of the sacraments in the Latin Church is well known, the Holy Communion is the principal locus of sanctification. Calvin expressly says that the Lord intended that the Holy Supper should "more forcefully than any other means quicken and inspire us both to purity and holiness of life, and to love, peace, and concord. For the Lord so communicates his body to us there that he is made completely one with us and we with him."[1] In the Reformed tradition, sanctification goes hand in hand with a sacramental churchmanship.

What, precisely, is the ideal of holiness in the Reformed tradition? Does it differ from that which prevails in say, Eastern Orthodoxy? There is no *radical* difference, of course, for in so far as any Christian[2] tradition is faithful to Christ, who is the Church's common and only Lord, it has already specified its ideal of sanctity. Nevertheless, as a Congolese Christian sees Christ black, a Japanese Christian finds Him slant-eyed, and a Swedish Christian takes Him to be blond, so the various doctrinal and ecclesial heritages within the Universal Church see Him variously, each in its own guise. Nor are these varieties of sanctity deviations from a norm; on the contrary, they are the expression of the richness of the reality of Christian holiness. If, as the Reformation Fathers so vehemently and even repetitiously insist, Christ is the One Head of the Body that is His Church, in Him men of all races and nations, Jew or Greek, Chinese or Indian, Scandinavian or Italian, have

[1] John Calvin, *Institutes of the Christian Religion,* IV, xvii, 38 (Ed. John T. McNeil; vol. 2. Philadelphia: Westminster Press, 1960), p. 1414 f.
[2] To avoid misunderstanding I wish to state that I do not take personal holiness to be by any means exclusively Christian; but I have confined my attention to Christian conceptions of it. These have, I believe, distinctive common ground. [Author].

their spiritual life. Each man who enjoys that life invests his beloved Lord with a character that expresses, not the whole life of Christ, but that peculiar facet among the infinite aspects of the life of Christ that the particular individual is able uniquely to express. So, as the Holy Spirit at Pentecost spoke to each man "in his own native language",[1] (Acts 11.8) and as each man invests the countenance of Christ with his own style of features, and the voice of Christ with his own style of speech, so each man brings forth the life of Christ in his own special, inimitable way. In this sense only can the heirs of the Reformation have a special ideal of Christian holiness.

Moreover, before I answer the question I have posed ("What is the ideal of holiness in the Reformed tradition?") I would ask the reader's forbearance while I make a few observations essential for an understanding of the Reformation heritage. The first point to be made is that the heirs of the Reformation are heirs also of the mediaeval Western or Latin tradition. They cannot abandon the latter tradition without at the same time abandoning their Reformation heritage, for the Reformation was nothing if not the reformation of the Catholic Church. As I have elsewhere pointed out,[2] it was as much a failure as it was a success in terms of its own aims. To understand what these aims were is essential, of course, to the understanding of what it means to be within the Reformation heritage and therefore of what the ideal of holiness is within the Reformed tradition. What is vulgarly called "Protestantism" is either Catholic or it is radically opposed to the fundamental aim of the Reformers, namely, the reformation of the Catholic Church.[3] Against the notion that "Protestantism" has a special gift for the spawning of sects and sectaries should be considered the fact that the Euchites, the Paulicians, the Bogomiles, the Albigenses, the Waldenses and the Brethren of the Free Spirit, were as much sectaries as have been any of the Reformation's offspring. There have been, indeed, "Protestant" sectaries who may be accounted as much and as little the children of the Reformation as were those others the children of Constantinople and Rome. I shall have something to say later on of

---

[1] When I playfully teased a beloved Italian colleague of mine, a devout Roman Catholic, with the old saw that the Blessed Virgin could not have announced Pio Nono's favourite doctrine in the terms reported, "Je suis l'Immaculée Conception", since she would presumably speak less peccable French, saying rather, "Je suis la Conçue sans tache", my colleague unhesitatingly and very properly retorted, "But our Lady would not talk French to a peasant like Bernadette; she would talk Béarnais; the fault is the French translator's."

[2] E.g. *Corpus Christi* (London: Macmillan, 1959) and *The Coming Reformation* (London: Hodder & Stoughton, 1960).

[3] It is true, however, that much modern "Protestantism" has wholly alienated itself from its own Reformation heritage.

ideals of sanctity among these heterodox heirs of the Reformation to whom, as to those in other traditions, Rufus Jones has shown, the Church is very much indebted.[1] Meanwhile I shall address myself to the subject within the Reformation heritage of the Catholic faith.

As I have already suggested, we are not to expect a radical deviation from the ideals of holiness that prevailed in those circles in mediaeval Latin Christendom, whose intellectual notions were inspired by figures such as St. Augustine and St. Thomas. We shall see points of difference rather than of contrast. We may first note, then, that the tendency in the Reformed tradition has always been against that kind of holiness that expresses itself in the mortification of the flesh for its own sake. Of course such an attitude to mortification has been disapproved among informed Roman Catholics both before and after Trent; nevertheless within the Roman tradition there has been sometimes a tolerance of self-inflicted physical austerities that has found no favour at all among Geneva's sons. The Reformation notion of holiness does indeed imply a readiness to suffer when suffering seems to be God's will; but in the Reformation heritage this aspect of sanctity has not been generally felt to be of the essence of personal holiness, being accounted, rather, as it was in the Stoic heritage to which St. Augustine and the whole Latin Church owed so much, a kind of natural fortitude that Christian men and women ought to cultivate in the course of the development of their inner life of holiness with Christ. Its role is more like the role that detachment and adaptability play in the life of an enterprising, faithful Jesuit missionary than it is a part of the process of personal sanctification.

What I have just been saying is in theory very close, of course, to post-Tridentine Roman Catholic teaching: no hair shirts for their own sake but only if they do in fact assist in the development of the interior life of personal sanctification. Yet in practice, as every Englishman is said to love a lord and every Hindu a *sunnyasi*, there is a strong popular tendency, among those little touched by the Reformation heritage, to admire external abstinences and mortifications as though they provided at least *presumptive* testimony to an interior life of growth in Christ if not proof of its attainment. In the Reformation heritage, however, such performances are, to say the least, suspect. Long before the development of modern psycho-analytical critiques, all preoccupation with instruments of physical mortification was regarded as in one way or another unhealthy and therefore unprofitable. Indeed, popular antipathy to external forms of asceticism has been so strong that it has often under-

[1] Rufus M. Jones, *The Church's Debt to Heretics*. (London: J. Clarke, 1925).

mined appreciation of certain types of holiness that have been traditionally admired in the Latin Church. "Protestants" are more likely to
be able to appreciate a St. Francis of Sales than a St. Paul of the Cross.
Their admiration for St. Francis of Assisi springs from the humane
qualities associated with that much-loved saint rather than from his
predilection for "Holy Poverty". Yet simplicity of life and a renuncia-
tion of worldly pomp and glory are eminently characteristic of the
Reformed tradition and play a large part in its calculus of sanctity.

The meaning of Reformed tradition

The term "Reformed tradition" may be understood in a wide or
narrow sense.

In the wide sense it would apply to every expression of Christian faith
and practice that owes its life to any of the series of changes that took
place in Western Christendom between the fourteenth and the seventeenth centuries and that together may be loosely designated as "the
Reformation". The term would then include, for instance, the Lutheran
Churches of Germany, Sweden and elsewhere, which owe their distinctive
ethos to the thought and action of Martin Luther (1483-1546). It would
also include the various Churches that make up the modern Anglican
communion, having their focus in Canterbury and their common heritage
in the Church of England, and preserving in a unique way the historic
Episcopate and Catholic ethos together with the Reformation heritage.

In the narrow and strict sense, however, which I shall follow here,
the term refers to those Churches that are specifically indebted to the
Genevan Reformation of which the French reformer, John Calvin
(1509-1564), was the leader. The Reformation in this form was very
articulate in its theology, dealing brilliantly with the fashionable
themes of the day. Its teachers stressed, for instance, the ancient notion,
expounded by St. Augustine and others, that a Christian's trials are
immeasurably lightened by the joy of interior assurance that by God's
infinite and incomprehensible grace and mercy he has been somehow
picked out (predestined) and earmarked (elected) for salvation, that is,
the enjoyment of God for ever. They also emphasised the general
Reformation theme that we are made right (justified) not by what we
do (e.g. pilgrimages and fasts) but by faith in Christ. With this doctrine
of "justification" went also a doctrine of "sanctification", the nature of
which I shall touch upon later.

The practical success of the Genevan Reformation was by no means commensurate with the intellectual respectability it acquired and has, in Christian theological circles, maintained. In France, then a very great world power and Calvin's natural terrain, it lost the opportunities the Lutheran and English Reformations enjoyed elsewhere. Repudiated in 1593 by the French king Henry IV, who thought Paris "worth a Mass", it lacked the means of showing what the Catholic Church, when reformed in Genevan style, could mean to a great nation.

Reformed Churches flourished, however, in various parts of continental Europe. In France the Huguenots were doughty representatives of the Genevan tradition; Calvinist ideas exerted considerable influence in England; a national Church in this tradition was established in the Netherlands in 1622; in other countries such as Hungary, Reformed Churches have flourished; and of course Reformed Churches abound in the United States, the British Commonwealth countries overseas, and elsewhere throughout the world. Perhaps the most striking success of the Genevan type of Reformation was in Scotland, where the Reformed Church, established by law in 1560, has ever since remained the national Kirk. A Presbyterian form of government, though eminently consonant with the polity of the Reformed Church, is by no means essential to it, and indeed the national Church of Scotland since 1560 has had more than one sort of episcopal government as well as the modern form of Presbyterianism that dates only from 1690 and was by no means precisely what the Scottish reformer John Knox (c. 1513-1572) had had in mind. The Church of Scotland is today, though independent of State control, officially established by law.[1]

The Queen, who is, of course, Head of the Church of England, is also, when she is in Scotland, a member of the national Kirk, which is non-Anglican and a classic exemplar of the family of Reformed Churches throughout the world. Among recent British sovereigns, Her Majesty has been, in fact, especially gracious in her personal recognition of the place of the Scottish Kirk in British tradition and life.

The Reformation heritage in America

The distinction the late Professor H. Richard Niebuhr of Yale used to make in his interpretation of "American Protestantism" between, on

[1] The Kirk has unfortunately suffered widespread deterioration in her power to appropriate her own heritage. The resulting decay of her ethos has been much hastened in recent decades by pressures, to which she is particularly susceptible, from sectarian and other special-interest groups. By so alienating herself from her own most valuable traditions she has naturally forfeited the esteem of Catholic-minded people that she once enjoyed both within and without her borders.

E

the one hand, the mediaeval Catholic emphasis on the perfection of God and man's contemplation and, on the other, the Reformer's stress on the sovereignty of God and man's service and activity, is applicable in some measure to the Reformation heritage in Europe as well as in America. Moreover, the United States today is so vast and variegated that almost nothing can be predicated of it. There is some truth, no doubt, in Perry Miller's remark that the American Puritans really had too little rather than too much sense of tragedy, and if they had too little, certainly their heirs did not have too much.[1] The Reformed heritage in America did lack the deep sacramental sense that in Europe the heirs of the Reformation had enjoyed. Today, however, the situation in America is so extremely complex and so highly ecumenical that no such statements have anything like the same contemporary application they may have once possessed. What is to be noticed in the United States today is that perhaps even more conspicuously than in contemporary Europe, the saint, in whatever tradition he may have been nurtured, is more detachable from it than was the case with the holy men of past ages within the Reformation heritage. The saint, as mystic, is also, however (and this is indeed an American phenomenon to be reckoned with) at once less likely to be at war with his ecclesiastical connection and less likely to be specifically grateful for it than has been traditionally the case with his European and British counterparts. Few Europeans sufficiently appreciate either the magnitude of the spiritual resources of the United States today or their prodigious vivacity. For all that, saints, though not extremely unusual, are certainly no commoner anywhere than they were before, nor could they be, since they constitute the spiritual aristocracy of mankind. By the same token, like every true aristocracy, they are not created overnight.

The nature of personal holiness

There is a very positive tendency in the Reformed tradition to regard personal holiness as a normal result of the life of every true believer rather than as an exceptional manifestation or distinctive wonder. Hence there is little liking for singling out and dubbing particular individuals as "saints". Not by accident is there no canonisation process in the Reformed Church. Canonisation proceedings, involving the official recognition by the Church of the sanctity of certain persons, would

---

[1] Quoted by William Lee Miller in "American Religion and American Political Attitudes" in James Ward Smith and A. Lelard Jamison (Eds.), *Religious Perspectives and American Culture* (Princeton University Press, 1961), p. 94.

ill suit the temper of the Reformed Church even if it involved no notion of degrees of recognition such as is made between the *beati* and the *sancti* in Roman practice. More distasteful still is the fact that any official recognition of sanctity suggests, even if it does not imply, that personal holiness is in some way a departure from the normal course of things, like a miraculous intervention of the hand of God in history rather than the normal ingathering of the harvest of those whom He has chosen for the immeasurable privilege of growth in holiness and grasp of eternal bliss.

A deeply religious friend of mine, a Scottish Presbyterian by birth who, after a long spiritual Odyssey that included a period of years among the Quakers and also a love for the Church of England, returned a few years ago to the Kirk of his fathers, is now devoting to it his years of retirement, as an active layman. When I asked him his personal views on holiness, his lengthy reply included the following remarks: "I am not attracted to the idea of people seeking *to obtain* holiness. When I say someone 'lives near to God' I mean he strikes me as living in constant direct consciousness of God rather than merely referring all matters to God by verbal prayer. But I do not mean that one can be taught how to achieve this relationship, which I should think is one of God's great gifts to his Beloved just as He might make a little girl's face sweet or give a young man a fine physique. I think 'evangelicals' of all Churches tend to strive too consciously to be good. They always feel apart from God and try to refer to Him as often as possible by prayer. I think a saintly person of any religion lives naturally and acts instinctively in the spirit of God. He does not have to make the conscious reference the 'evangelicals' do. I do not believe in extraordinary Christians. We are *all* 'called to be saints'; therefore sanctity cannot be a special condition to be realised by exceptional people. Holiness or sanctity means a growing and increasing conformity to what God reveals of His own character, and therefore it can never be defined." My correspondent thinks these views may sound heretical for a son of the Kirk; but I believe they are, on the contrary, both deeply Catholic in spirit and full of Reformation emphasis.

That there are tares as well as wheat in the fields of God's Church is well recognised by all who are in the mainstream of the Reformed tradition. The wheat is expected to produce a consistently good quality of bread, and if there should be some particularly outstanding crops,

---

[1] I must add, however, that since I wrote these words, he has been unable to find a spiritual home in the Kirk of his fathers and has become a Scottish Episcopal layman.

the difference between them and the normally good bread is less noteworthy than the fact that there is a regular harvest of golden grain produced by God on terrain the Devil had made his hunting ground.

When we think of people who have the sure marks of having walked with God and of having attained spiritual triumph, we think first of a host of relatives and friends, people we have known intimately. We rejoice in their companionship and support, on either side of the veil that separates the Church Militant from the Church Triumphant. Aunt Bessie and Cousin Bob are likely to be much more real to most people than Cosmas and Damian or even St. Gregory of Nyssa. The "Protestant" is inclined to ask why he should concern himself with distant personages, even if they be not legendary or historically obscure, in order to find a figure to symbolise patience, joy, charity or any other fruit of the Holy Spirit, when, from his own immediate environment, his own sister or grandfather may be a far more obvious and striking exemplar. The "Protestant" is sometimes in danger of losing that historical perspective that can bring a deep and wonderful awareness of the vastness of God's family; but in his concern with known instances of personal holiness he is, to say the least, very much on the right track. He has before him visible examples of what it is to be holy, and the acute awareness of this makes him tend to suspect the practice of "naming" saints.

For such reasons no attempt to establish a calendar of saints among the heirs of the Reformation would be likely to meet with approval even if it could meet with success. The hesitancy to talk about saints is more than mere reticence, though it may sometimes have this as its concomitant; it springs from a definite and lively dislike of the suggestion that a vocation to a life of personal holiness is something extremely unusual, like a vocation to join the Trappists or to become a Camaldolese hermit. Even discriminations in sanctity based upon distinctions such as one can see between the special heroism of the martyr or "pioneer" in the faith and the more dogged but less lustrous heroism of the faithful servant who simply accepts his daily burden for Christ are hardly in keeping with the mind of the Reformed Church. In this tradition one does not care to make any such distinctions radical. After all, if there is a calculus for personal holiness at all (and such a notion is by no means alien to the Reformed tradition), the dramatic or spectacular is least likely to be the proper basis for it. A lifetime of quiet endurance out of love for and fidelity to a friend may be surely more glorious in the sight of heaven than even the fiery stake which St. Augustine thought so special that it qualified as baptism "by blood".

That there are degrees of holiness is not by any means contrary to the teaching of the Reformers, who were one with St. Augustine in seeing that "Inchoate[1] love . . . is inchoate holiness; advanced love is advanced holiness; great love is great holiness."[2] Yet in the Reformed heritage this recognition is in a way akin to the recognition we give to degrees of intelligence or degrees of cleanliness: our recognition of such degrees is in practice so overshadowed by our gratitude at discovering intelligence and our satisfaction in finding cleanliness that we hardly care to say very much about gradations. Sanctity, the spiritual flower, is to be acclaimed whether in bud or in bloom. When the snowdrop bursts out of the hard earth we do not compare sizes. And how, indeed, should one compare the personal holiness of delicate Aunt Bessie with that of boisterous Cousin Bob, or of either with that of St. Catherine dei Ricci?

Some classic types

For all that, there are indeed certain figures in the Reformed Church who have come down in history as distinctive instruments of God in the fulfilment of his purposes. In our own time, too, one's mind naturally turns to such remarkable men as Albert Schweitzer (1875-1965), who gave his extraordinary intellectual genius to medical missionary service in Africa. The Lutheran-born Dietrich Bonhoeffer (1906-1945), a young German theologian executed in a Nazi prison camp, who has become, like Karl Barth and Martin Niemöller, a great examplar of the spirit of Germany's "Confessing Church" (*Bekennende Kirche*), is also the kind of figure that is especially admired in the Reformed tradition. In the nineteenth century, which was one of extensive missionary work in Africa and elsewhere, innumerable names come to mind such as that of Mary Slessor (1848-1915), a Scottish mill girl who, turned missionary, gained great Christian influence over the African tribe among which she laboured, where she succeeded in abolishing human sacrifice, twin murder and other forms of ritual cruelty. In missionaries like David Livingstone (1813-1873) and Mary Slessor, and in martyrs such as Bonhoeffer, there is a heroic quality that has been much admired in

[1] By what the translator renders "inchoate" St. Augustine meant what we might call "immature".

[2] St. Augustine, *On Nature and Grace*, c. 84, in *Basic Writings of Saint Augustine* (Ed. Whitney J. Oates; vol. 1; New York: Random House, 1948), p. 579.

the Reformed tradition, since the early struggles of the Reformers entailed many sufferings that had to be endured for the Faith. Prominent in Scottish Reformation hagiography, for instance, is the proto-martyr Patrick Hamilton (*c.* 1504-1528), a young gentleman and scholar, who was burned at the stake with exceptional cruelty. The popularity of the English Calvinist John Foxe's (1516-1587) sixteenth-century account of the cruel sufferings of "Protestants" in England under Mary Tudor (1516-1558) was due to more than the morbidity often associated with interest in such vivid descriptions. Those nurtured in the principles of the Reformation were well accustomed to the notion that God's purpose for the reform of Christ's Church would not come about without sufferings hardly less terrible than those suffered by earlier Christians under Nero and Diocletian. The Christian life is in essence heroic, and the Christian saint truly a hero. There was no need, in the sixteenth century, to seek out hair shirts and other appurtenances of mediaeval penance: anyone truly living in the Christian Faith was bound to receive all the buffeting and pain he could need for the attainment of personal holiness. Nor has there seemed, in later ages, much need for rules of fasting amohg those inured to the tradition of "low living and high thinking" that has adorned so many manses and other Christian homes within the Reformed Church.

Yet when we come to consider whether the type of holiness characteristically revered in the Reformed tradition is that of the heroic confessor or martyr, we find this is by no means the case. Indeed, by looking instead at another strain of saint we might be tempted to reach the no less erroneous conclusion that the gentle, sweet and amiable type of personality is the one most admired within the Reformation heritage. Of the innumerable exemplars of this type of piety may be mentioned, very arbitrarily, of course, Mary Duncan (1814-1840), daughter of Robert Lundie, Minister of Kelso, in whose features her friends are said to have seen a close resemblance to the portraits of Madame Guyon, and whose hymns, written for her own children, exhibit her rare amiability and tenderness. The English Puritans, on the other hand, whose inheritance was from Geneva, though from the standpoint of their Scottish and continental European brethren they sometimes lost the broad humanity and deep churchmanship that belongs to the Genevan tradition, provide celebrated examples of another type of piety that is also splendid in its way.

John Bunyan (1628-1688) is an obvious example, from the English side of the border, of a poor man's son who, fired with a love for the

English Bible, was so influenced by the beauty and power of its style that he was able to produce great works of his own, at least one of which, *The Pilgrim's Progress*, is so matchless in the simplicity of its prose and the earnestness of its message that no one can easily doubt the sanctity of the man who wrote it.

No type of saintliness, however, has been more beloved among Geneva's heirs than that which combines humane learning with Christian zeal. The Scottish tradition has especially favoured the humane type of saint who, being so intimate with God that he is at ease with all men, sinner and saint, seems awesomely winsome to the former, curiously appealing to the latter, yet always demanding towards himself. Robert Leighton (1611-1684), Archbishop of Glasgow, belongs to the Reformation heritage. The greater part of his devotional works were written while he was Minister of Newbattle and on the Presbyterian side of the fierce battle that raged within the Kirk in seventeenth-century Scotland between those who favoured an episcopal and those who wished a presbyterian form of government for the Church of Scotland. His influence over a remarkably diversified group of great men, such as Coleridge and Döllinger, Gladstone and Martineau, Wesley and Lord Morley, attests the universality of his appeal. At the present ecumenically-minded time, he has become a symbol of meekness and reconciliation.

Richard Baxter (1615-1691), author of *The Saints' Everlasting Rest*, for long a popular English devotional classic, is a person whose type of sanctity readily commands, within the Reformed tradition, the deepest sympathy and admiration. In the hideous turmoils of seventeenth-century ecclesiastical strife, when differences between Anglicans and Presbyterians were acute, Baxter, who suffered persecution under the notorious Judge Jeffreys, sought as far as possible to ignore (as his contemporary unsuccessfully sought to reconcile) these differences in an age when differences were sharpened by many on both sides. His pastoral devotion is well attested, and his quiet, firm resistance to what he believed to be court frivolity and ecclesiastical corruption is very congenial to the temper of the Reformed Church which, while by no means necessarily opposed to either bishops or kinds, has been vehemently and insistently disdainful of political irresponsibility of every kind.

Those whose naturally passionate and impetuous disposition God has disciplined to His own service are by no means without a place in the Reformed tradition, and the lovable Samuel Rutherford (*c.* 1600-1661) is a fitting representative of this type. Because of a pre-marital indiscretion he was deprived of a professorial chair in Humanity at Edinburgh University, to which he had been appointed in his early twenties. Thereafter he became deeply religious and strongly Calvinistic. His letters express in an inimitable way his extraordinarily intimate sense of the presence of Christ. There is a curious joy in some of his turns of phrase. For example: "I am bank and brim full: a great high springtide of the consolations of Christ hath overwhelmed me." The passionate language he uses has shocked and even nauseated many; yet the appeal others find in him sufficiently establishes him as a true master of the spiritual life. For all his tendency to sentimentality, which some have found cloying, he is constantly ready to urge himself and others, as he beseeches a friend in one of his many remarkable letters, "to make sure work of salvation". This insistence on the idea that the Christian is engaged in *work* is very characteristic of the type of sanctity most admired in the Reformed tradition. Whether Christ is seen dimly beyond the gates of heaven, as in Bunyan, or as a constant, daily companion, as in Rutherford, there is no question of what the Christian must be about: he is about his Master's business, which is no less work for being a work of love. To play at religion is to be a hypocrite. Feeling is, of course, important, yet too much preoccupation with it is dangerously near playing at religion. The saints are always workers for God.

George Whitefield says that a little book Charles Wesley put into his hands so affected him that whenever in later life he went to Oxford he could not help running to the place where, through the treatise it contained, Christ, he said, had first revealed Himself to him. The book, which is indeed a very brief one, was Henry Scougal's (1650-1678) *Life of God in the Soul of Man*, published in 1677. Scougal, son of Patrick Scougal, Bishop of Aberdeen, spent some years, after a brief period of teaching philosophy at King's College, Aberdeen, as Minister of Auchterless. He then returned to Aberdeen, serving for the rest of his life in a chair of theology. The notion of sanctity that is presented in his solitary opuscule is conformable to the main tradition of Scottish piety and to the characteristic ideas on the interior life that are to be found in Greek and Latin Fathers such as Chrysostom and Ambrose. Though described on a monument as "eager for heaven", he was rather a man whose awareness of the interior life was so strong that he was able to bring heaven into the faithful performance of the chores of everyday life, investing duty with love and imbuing all around him with a sense of his own debt to God's free grace. Such piety is very close to the mind and heart of the Scottish heritage, of which he is such a fine ornament.

So venerated for his sanctity was William Guthrie (1620-1665) of
Fenwick that when the Archbishop of Glasgow suspended him in 1664
during the bitter struggles between Bishop and Presbyter, no clergyman
could be found who would publicly announce the sentence. He is said
to have been remarkable both for his extraordinary reverence in
prayer and for his irrepressible love of fun. William Guthrie's friends
noticed that his fun seemed to come from a mysterious, inexhaustible
source. When he told his hearers to praise God, some growled that they
had nothing to praise Him for; but Guthrie blithely told them to
praise Him for the good weather and for bringing sunshine to the lambs
in the field. His spiritual classic, *The Christian's Great Interest*, which made
its first appearance in 1659, passed through many editions and was
translated into French, German and other languages. It is often quaint
to modern ears. For instance, he who in a sermon counselled his hearers
"Do not difficult the way to Heaven", tells his readers that if only they
will come to Christ, Christ will welcome them, and he asks: "Is it a
matter of such intricacy and insuperable difficulty, greedily to look to
that exalted Saviour?" And yet the unmistakable insistence upon
struggle that is inseparable from the Reformed tradition of spirituality
is there too: "They complain that they know not whether they be in
Christ or not; but as few take pains to be in Him, so few take pains
to try if they be in Him. It is a work and business which cannot be done
sleeping." Some might wonder fearfully whether they were among those
whom God had chosen for salvation. There is an easy way of finding
out: "God excludes none, if they do not exclude themselves." How lovely
are the doctrines of predestination, election and assurance on the lips
of the saints, and how odious are they when interpreted by those who
have never experienced God's grace!

Mirth is very close to the Kingdom of God, and I believe its absence
is an unmistakable mark of the absence of sanctity. The charge that
Geneva engenders mirthlessness is indeed a radical indictment of the
Reformed Church which, if justified, would make her a promising
candidate for the role of Antichrist. The saints, whatever the soil in
which their sanctity has been nurtured, and however different their
Christian style, have one quality in common: they are full of fun.
Several reasons for this might be suggested; but one seems to me
sufficient: the road to sanctity is so hard and the danger of self-
consciousness so great and so fatal, that without a peculiarly vivacious
sense of humour nobody could even get to first base. Indeed, I think one
must go so far as to say that nowhere is the mystical indwelling of God

in the souls of His Saints more plainly manifested in the empirical world than in the laughter that is the expression of saintly merriment. Yeats has noticed that "the good are always the merry"; but the distinctive merriment of the holy is more scintillating than any other kind. They laugh as if God Himself were laughing not only with them but in them and sometimes also even at them.

Zachary Boyd (c. 1590-1664), to whom English-speaking heirs of the Reformation owe the first line of the beautiful metrical version of the twenty-third Psalm ("The Lord's my Shepherd, I'll not want"),[1] has the same characteristic insistence on "working at" one's relations with God. "Heaven is not winne with a wish," he writes quaintly in *The Last Battell of the Soul*, published in 1629, which treats of the death-bed battle of the soul with Satan, who makes a final bid to finish his unholy war against it by seducing it at the last moment from its attachment to God.

In every tradition the saints have often been suspect of heresy during their lives. This is inevitable, because of the close connection between sanctity and mysticism, which is nowhere more evident than in the Reformed tradition. Those who after death have been accounted classic exponents of the orthodoxy of their tradition have been, in their lifetime, sometimes under a cloud, as was St. Thomas, for example, before he attained his position as a quasi-official exponent of Roman Catholic teaching. In Scotland, at a time when many in the Kirk had fallen into an aridly dogmatic form of nineteenth-century Calvinism, a young parish minister, John MacLeod Campbell (1800-1872), was deposed from the ministry by the General Assembly of the Church in 1831 for teaching that Christ died for all men. This was held to be contrary to the confessional standards of the Kirk, and the approved theological opinion of the day, according to which the correct interpretation of Reformed Church doctrine was that Christ died only for the elect.[2] Campbell had become convinced, in or about 1826, of the universality of the Atonement, to which teaching he conjoined a strong emphasis on the doctrine of assurance. His heresy trial shocked many and became memorable not only because his teaching eventually prevailed (his later book on the Atonement came to be used in the Scottish theological colleges), but more especially because of Campbell's conspicuous personal holiness. Campbell's own flock in the then remote and

---

[1] Millar Patrick, *Four Centuries of Scottish Psalmody* p. 103. (London: O.U.P., 1949).
[2] This is incompatible however with several texts in Calvin, who says, for example, in his *Commentary on Matt.* xxvi. 28: "Sub multorum nomine non partem mundi tantum designat, sed totum humanum genus." Cf. his *Commentary on Romans*, v. 18.

beautiful little West Highland parish of Row (now spelt Rhu), when they had heard of the initiation of proceedings against him in the ecclesiastical courts, sent in a formal petition "unto the Venerable the General Assembly", signed by 420 persons, representing 95 per cent of all the inhabitants of the parish. In this they expressed their profound gratitude for "having so zealous and holy man as their minister", and earnestly prayed that he might not be taken away from them.

Campbell represented a scholarly type of Scottish parish minister. Better read in the Greek and Latin Fathers than were most of his Scottish contemporaries, he was acquainted with the writings of English divines such as Latimer, Becon and Jewel, in whom he found support for his doctrine, and was plainly a more careful student of Calvin than were his accusers and judges. In later years he counted Kingsley, Maurice, and the future Cardinal Manning among his friends.[1] When charges, set forth in more than 180 pages, were being formulated against him in Presbytery, he found time, in the midst of compiling careful theological answers to them, to write a note to his father, telling him serenely that the case had already been "substantially decided" against him, which note he signed "abiding in the peace of God and the secret of the Lord's presence at Dumbarton at the Presbytery bar". More than one Scottish divine in later years recalled that when one talked with Campbell one felt a strange sense of the presence of a "Third Being". He was indeed a saint. Some of the Scottish crofters might have called him "far ben with God".[2]

Among those who warmly took up Campbell's cause after the latter's deposition was Thomas Erskine of Linlathen (1788-1870), a very unusual religious thinker. Erskine was a lawyer who, on succeeding to family estates, gave up the Scottish Bar to devote himself to the study of theology. His often highly original thought is expressed in a curiously haunting style. That in the service of God is perfect freedom is a characteristic theme of Erskine's and seems to have motivated his indubitably holy life. The language he uses about the necessity of having a "Thou" rather than a "He" relationship with God prefigures that of the "I-Thou" theology associated with the late Martin Buber.[3] Erskine

[1] His son took Holy Orders in the Church of England, and his grandson became a Canon of Westminster.

[2] A crofter's cottage was sometimes called a "butt and ben": the butt was the public room and the "ben" the private apartment. Only intimate friends of the family would be asked to "come ben", and to be "far ben" with anyone was to be on terms of close kinship with him. To call anyone "far ben with God" was to designate him a saint.

[3] Martin Buber told me in Jerusalem a few months before his death that the fundamental idea he had eventually developed into his *Ich und Du* had come to him in the German trenches during the First World War.

insisted, like Kierkegaard, on the uncompromising character of Christianity. He is said to have had a great gift for friendship – a gift that is typical of the saint in every tradition.

In the Scottish tradition of piety, which was for centuries rooted in a daily life of family prayer as well as in a lengthy hebdomadal exercise of public worship, the idea of saintliness was so deeply present that one was expected to note it rather than talk about it. In the language and demeanour of some men and women was a very beautiful and mysterious quality. They *glowed*; but the glow was a quiet, interior glow as if their faces were equipped with what today's camera-men would call "rear-lighting". They had the same passions as other men and women, the same differences in temperament (such as Victoria Sackville-West has contrasted in her well-known study of the two Teresas),[1] and the same differences in taste and style; yet it seemed as though something inside them had been in every case dipped in a special spiritual fragrance. This they exuded, especially in animated conversation, just as lavender works its way through the pores of its container. I have never had any difficulty in understanding what the hagiographers of the Latin tradition mean when they write of people who die *in odore sanctitatis*, for I recognise at once in the phrase an allusion to the spiritual fragrance I was accustomed from an early age to note without comment in a considerable number of elderly people. I was no more expected to talk about it than my Victorian parents would have talked about sexuality; but one was no less aware of it than were the Victorians of that more general phenomenon.

Perhaps there was in all this something of a notion that has a distinctive role in Eastern Orthodox spirituality, namely, the transfiguration of the human being into a new creature. If so, there was certainly no explicit teaching of it. On the contrary, so marked was the disinclination even to allude to holiness that I am not at all sure how I ever came to "perceive" the quality I am calling spiritual fragrance. All I know is that in my recollections of early childhood awareness, which happen to be vivid, this "perception" is quite distinct. I can remember the sharp distinction I somehow learned to draw between what I might now call, for convenience, the "formal" sanctity of a clergyman *qua* clergyman and the "real" sanctity of a human being, clerical or lay, and I think the making of this distinction in some way helped me to "perceive' what I am now calling "real sanctity", evidenced by the "spiritual fragrance". All I know is that the incidence of the phenomenon was

[1] V. Sackville-West, *The Eagle and the Dove*, London: Michael Joseph, 1943.

confined, in my experience, to elderly people, and of course to only a small number of these.

That charming Edinburgh divine W. P. Paterson quoted approvingly in his Gifford Lectures the remark of his colleague A. E. Taylor that "the lives of the saints are the real answer of Theism to the last insistent perplexities of the doubter who lurks in all of us".[1]

Special traditions

We may now come to consider some of the special traditions which, while making no claim to be that reform of the Catholic Church that the Genevan Fathers sought, are nevertheless in one way or another connected with that heritage. They are numerous, both in England, which a disgruntled French observer once called a land of a hundred religions and only one sauce, and in America, where more than 250 Christian bodies report statistics annually to the *Yearbook of American Churches*, from which figure are excluded many smaller yet interesting sects and groups. I can only take a few examples, and while some readers may find the selection obvious others will account it arbitrary.

The Congregationalist and Baptist traditions

There are in the English-speaking world many churches which, though associated in unions, groups or other confederations, insist upon government by the local congregation rather than by an episcopal jurisdiction as in the Church of England or by a hierarchy of ecclesiastical courts as in the Presbyterian form of government adopted by the Church of Scotland. Their history is long and complicated. Here the simplest indications must suffice. The spirit of modern Congregationalists and Baptists, for all the extremely wide variety of outlook between them and within each group, is that of the seventeenth-century English Separatists, though both have more ancient roots. Their prevailing conception of the Church is that of a series of local and separate or independent congregations. In this they differ from those who sought to avoid sectarianism and to achieve the "Catholic Church Reformed", whether in the Scottish style or, *modo anglicano*, in the Church of England.

---

[1] W. P. Paterson, *The Nature of Religion* (Second edition: Gifford Lectures 1924-25; London: Hodder & Stoughton, 1928), p. 496.
Paterson, a Church of Scotland clergyman, was Dean of Divinity in the University of Edinburgh; Taylor, an Anglican layman, was Professor of Moral Philosophy in the same university.

As early as the seventeenth century Calvinist doctrine had already deeply affected many in both groups. In the seventeenth century the situation in England was so confused that it is impossible to make any neat classification. That is why I have been able to cite John Bunyan, for instance, as a very obvious heir of the Genevan Reformation, though he was in fact an outstanding figure among the English Separatists, advocating a system of local fellowships that would include what we may now call Congregationalists and Baptists.

Puritanism in England and New England

Those persons in England who, dissatisfied with the Elizabethan Settlement, wanted the English Church modelled after a stricter Genevan pattern, came to be called Puritans – a designation that ceased to be appropriate after 1660. Their influence was both deep and widespread. The Geneva Bible, for instance, went through sixty editions in Elizabeth's reign, though it never had her official approval. It was the Bible of Shakespeare. It was the Bible of the Pilgrim Fathers, who brought to the American colonies the Puritan influence that was to play an immense role in their religious, social and cultural development. In both England and Scotland, however, and certainly not least in Ireland, the politico-religious regime of Oliver Cromwell (1599-1658) left memories so odious that the Puritan tradition with which it was associated lost favour in the British Isles. For all that, Puritans deeply affected both English and American notions of sanctity.

A struggle between the claims of humane learning and the commitment of a Christian to New Testament teaching and practice had vexed the early Christian Fathers and troubled the mediaeval Latin Church. It now appeared once again in New England. There, in the midst of the movement called the Great Awakening (1740-1743), Jonathan Edwards (1703-1758) tried to discriminate between the healthy and the unhealthy elements in the controversy. His remarks on holiness give us a clue to the ideals of the Christian society to which he belonged. "Holiness," he writes, "appeared to me to be of a sweet, charming, serene, calm nature; which brought an inexpressible purity, brightness, peacefulness and ravishment to the soul." Against those who expected conversion experiences to issue in great emotional outbursts, such as heaving and moaning, Edwards and others sought to encourage a more restrained and sedate expectation.

Some saints may be emotional, as some saints may be Scandinavian;

but sanctity no more consists in an emotional quality that it consists in the quality of being Danish. Sanctity is an interior state, beginning with an interior gift and issuing in a fruit which, springing from a quiet, luminous serenity within, shines out into the actions and even, it may be, the very countenance of the saint. This does not mean that we can measure the holiness of a saint by the amount of luminosity in his face! Nevertheless, the luminous quality may have something to do with the halo or nimbus that conventionally adorns the heads of the saints in representational art. Certainly, saintliness is not to be identified with any particular kind of human behaviour such as could ever be casually imitated. Any actress worth her salt can pretend to be in love; any skilful barrister can affect indignation; all politicians sound patriotic; but no one but a saint can pass for a saint among people who have ever known a real one. The Puritan tradition is especially emphatic about this. Sanctity cannot be counterfeited, for though it is found in the least expected places it is inimitable. Henry James has a short story, "The Real Thing", about an artist who, unable to make his picture of an elegant couple convincing when he modelled it from a couple who were in fact "the real thing" in terms of their breeding and education did much better with Miss Churm who, being "only a freckled cockney", couldn't spell and sometimes looked "a trifle blowsy", yet "could represent anything from a fine lady to a shepherdess". What is distinctive about sanctity is that it cannot be represented at all except in an extremely formal and conventional fashion, as, for example, with the halo. Any good mimic can represent Charlie Chaplin or Winston Churchill or Napoleon, because the peculiar qualities that make up such very distinctive personalities are such as, in some small measure, we all possess. No one could mimic the unique quality of an individual saint. Not even another saint could do it; nor indeed could he want to do it, for to try would be like a ruby trying to mimic an emerald or a lily a rose.

The Quaker tradition

Of all the heirs of the Genevan Reformation who deviated from its ecclesiological mainstream and attracted other alien influences, the Quakers are perhaps the most interesting and certainly not the least distinctive group. Historically associated with English Puritanism, yet distinguished in several ways from it in spirit, the Quakers were at first drawn mainly from the lower classes of seventeenth-century England. Before the Toleration Act of 1689, the savage whippings and other cruelties they suffered were more than matched by their extraordinary courage and fortitude in enduring them. They were especially vulnerable to persecution, for unlike other English sectaries they refused to meet in secret. Their founder, George Fox (1624-1691), came to feel that the Inner Light of the Living Christ that is in every man is every man's supreme spiritual authority and guide, for in it the very truth of God is directly communicated to each individual soul. Fox and the early Quakers recognised Scripture and "the sense of the Meeting" as also weighty authorities, though not to be compared to the supreme authority that every man carries within himself. The name "Quaker" was first applied to George Fox by Justice Bennet in 1650, by way of nickname, because Fox bade Bennet tremble at the Word of the Lord. The Quakers called themselves Friends of the Truth. The modern designation "Society of Friends" dates from no earlier than 1800. In the eighteenth century they had already developed marked peculiarities in dress and speech.

Quakers, because of the nature of the movement, have been for long unusually liable to oddities and aberrations. So today, though most Quakers are extreme pacifists (some even refuse to pay that portion of their Income Tax assessment that is to be spent on war), there are a few who deviate even from this norm. Though Quakers traditionally have disdained all "hireling ministries", there is an increasing use of paid ministers among them. There are even some who use the sacraments, though Quakers have generally done without these, accounting them unnecessary and even a possible barrier to direct inner communion with God.

In the United States there are some old-fashioned Quaker meeting-houses, especially in Pennsylvania, where the teachings as well as the spirit of Fox are closely followed; but the influence of Elias Hicks (1748-1830) and others who denied the need for traditional orthodox doctrine, encouraged many Friends to think of Christ simply as a very holy man and to allow all edifying literature, whether it be Milton or Wordsworth or the Bhagavad-gītā, as much and as little authority as canonical Scripture. In spite of the great diversity of outlook, however, and the fact that the Society nowadays tends to be a refuge for mystically-inclined people who have become disaffected from their own traditions, there is still a remarkably uniform spirit, an immense love for mankind that expresses itself in a "concern" to help wronged or underprivileged individuals and groups in very practical ways, and above all a deep respect for every man as holy by virtue of his having the "seed of God" within him. A Pennsylvania Quaker told me of a "concern", at one of the meetings on the eve of the Second World War, to send a friendly deputation to Hitler (than whom no man could be more abhorrent to a Quaker) in hope that he, having the "seed of God" within him, would work instead for peace. The deputation duly went, was received, and returned to report gravely to the meeting that "a way could not be found". Such is the faith of Quakers in the goodness of man. The Quaker ideal of holiness has never strayed from that of Fox who, when an armed man demanded that he come forth, came forth quietly in his familiar wide white hat, long coat and leather breeches, with the words, "Here I am, Friend," calmly approaching within three paces of the raised pistol of his adversary and escaping death by the power of love.

In a children's book that expresses with fine simplicity a characteristic Quaker view of the nature of sanctity, the author tells in an introductory chapter of a little Quaker girl who wondered why there were no saints in the windows of the Meeting House such as she had seen in English parish churches, and who found out later that saints are "real" windows because the sunshine with which they are filled even when they are doing dreary tasks simply "cannot help streaming out over the dull part and making it interesting".[1] The same child also gathered that a bad temper is the worst obstacle to becoming a saint, for she had heard her nurse say "it's enough to vex a saint"; but she discovered "What a number of things it does seem to take to make a Saint! But then it takes eggs and milk and butter and sugar and flour and currants and raisins too, to make a cake."[2]

Martyrdom was common among the early Quakers, and the Quaker martyrs and confessors are admired for their patience, a virtue always much esteemed among Friends. Yet perhaps even nearer the root of sanctity, on the Quaker view, is the quality of those mild men who, the Gospel promises, "shall inherit the earth".[3] (No doubt that special admiration for mildness is what had given the little Quaker girl the notion that a bad temper is the worst sin.) James Parnell, the first Quaker martyr, displays mildness throughout his terrible sufferings. The first Quakers to be publicly flogged in England were two women, Elizabeth Williams and Mary Fisher. They were ordered by the Mayor of Cambridge to be taken to the Market Cross and whipped "till the

[1] L. V. Hodgkin, *A Book of Quaker Saints* (London: Macmillan, 1922; first ed. 1917), p. 17.
[2] *Op. cit.*, p. 13f.
[3] Wyclif rendered the third beatitude "Blessed be the mylde men." The New English Bible has "How blest are those of a gentle spirit." Matt. v. 5.

F

blood ran down" their naked backs. The women knelt down on the ground to beseech the Lord to forgive the Mayor, because he could not have known what he was doing. After they had been led back through the town, their flesh torn by lashes administered as to the worst criminals, they exhorted the bystanders to fear God only, not man. Great is the Quaker fearlessness of human tyrants, and in no century has its awesome power been more needed than in our own! Nothing is more disdained by Quakers than servility. Christian meekness or mildness, they have had good reason to learn, is anything but submissiveness. It is always conjoined to that lack of fear of mere men that springs from being willing to quake only before Him who is the fount of all holiness. We who today are too much inclined to think that a "God-fearing" man or woman sounds a dreary and straitlaced character have forgotten that by fearing only God the saints of every age alone show no fear of men and for that reason know a freedom denied to others.

I asked one of my former students, Dr. David Le Shana, a Quaker who is now President of George Fox College, Oregon, for his view of the Quaker conception of sanctity. He summed it up as follows: "Holiness of life and character is not only a hoped-for goal of life, but is taught as being both practical and necessary. This sanctity is not so much a result of man's doing, however, as it is the work of God in man. It is instantaneous as well as progressive. Sanctification occurs not only as an act of God in time, it is also the process of God's continual dealing with man and man's response to His grace."

The Methodist Tradition

The movement that owes its origin to John Wesley (1703-1791) has played an important role in England since the last decades of the eighteenth century. Its influence on American religious life, though in some ways different, has been also very noteworthy. The Methodist Church is today the largest single Christian body in the United States other than the Roman Catholic Church, though the various Baptist bodies, taken together, are numerically greater. Methodism, though historically an offshoot of the Church of England, may be properly treated here. Various circumstances have for long brought Methodists into association with the heirs of the Genevan Reformation, notwithstanding that (a) most, though not all, Methodism has been anti-Calvinist in doctrine; (b) American Methodism has a strongly episcopal form of government; and (c) the spirit and tone of Methodism are in some ways closer to the Evangelical wing of the Church of England than to Geneva.

John Wesley, in his earlier years, assigned a very important place in his system to the notion of Christian perfection. Methodist writers have traditionally taught that some time after conversion another experience is to be expected, "the Great Salvation". Through this experience the Christian becomes convinced that all his sin has been completely and finally extinguished and he is restored to the very image of God. Wesley insisted that all his followers should always be aiming at this state of sanctity. Though the "Great Salvation" experience is apparently expected to be instantaneous and the gift of God, the process of sancti-fication through which it is fully appropriated and to which all genuine Christian growth must always tend, may be slow.

Bishop Gerald Kennedy, whom I have consulted as a prominent American Methodist churchman of my acquaintance, tells me that while only a minority of Methodists today take seriously enough the traditional doctrine of sanctification, a Methodist bishop must ask every aspirant to the full ministry of the Methodist Church who comes to him, "Are you going on to perfection?" and "Do you expect to be made perfect in love in this life?"

Traditionally, the perfected Methodist, though he is not accounted beyond the possibility of sin and wrong choice, should be able to pray incessantly in the sense that he is completely filled with the love of God. In theory the Methodist ideal of sanctity might seem to have affinities with that of the Salesian tradition in French Catholicism, which stresses *pur amour*. In practice the affinity is, to say the least, obscure.

The Salvationist Tradition

If Methodism be the daughter of the Church of England, Salva-tionism may perhaps claim to be her grand-daughter, for its founder, William Booth (1829-1912), whose family was partly Jewish, became a Methodist preacher and brought into his preaching much of the special accent of Methodism. Wesley had found the eighteenth-century English Church lacking in evangelical spirit and fervour; now his nineteenth-century followers found Booth more revivalistic than they could tolerate.

Salvationism, from Booth's founding of the Salvation Army in 1865, greatly stressed personal holiness. Though one would expect, and in many ways one finds, a great difference between the ethos of Quakers and that of Salvationists, they resemble each other in at least two points: a general rejection of the sacraments and an immense devotion to corporal works of mercy, such as feeding the hungry, redeeming the captive, and succouring the victims of oppression and war. The Salvationists see themselves, however, as committed to a holy war against human sin and as enlisted in an army whose task is to fight it. Their officers, regularly commissioned in this army, constitute the Salvationist counterpart of the clergy of other Churches.

I have elsewhere suggested[1] that the early Jesuits were a sort of mediaeval Salvation Army. As the Franciscans had begun as bookless mendicants in the thirteenth century and had become by the end of the same century one of the greatest intellectual forces in Europe, so the Jesuits, beginning as a seemingly quixotic band of knights of the Blessed Virgin, pledged to fight chivalrously for her honour and the exaltation of Mother Church, ended by becoming celebrated teachers, counting among their number the Church's most learned men. The Salvation Army, unlike Loyola's sixteenth-century Company or Society of Jesus, has not so far been transformed in that way, and no doubt, like all movements, it has lost some of the fervour of its early leaders; but it has certainly retained a distinctive conception of sanctity in which, as one would expect, the notion of the Church as an army is dominant. For Salvationists the Church is nothing if not militant.

This does not mean, of course, that the Quaker virtues of meekness and patience are unappreciated. On the contrary, the early Salvationists had plenty of opportunity to exercise them. Their patience was sorely tried. Though in the less savagely cruel climate of Victorian England they were not publicly whipped through the streets, as had been the Quakers, they also met ferocious opposition from both Church and State. At their open-air meetings, rotten eggs, garbage and dung were thrown in their faces as their eyes were closed in prayer, and sometimes a practical joker would creep behind a circle of Salvationists, tie the hands of all of them together, and then, when they discovered their plight, lead the jeers of the crowd. Ridicule and contempt, sometimes instigated by the parish clergy, were poured on these pioneers of what was to become a powerful evangelistic force for the Church and one of the most successful and beneficent agencies of social reform ever seen in the English-speaking world. A saint in this tradition is expected to be above all a soldier and so when a Salvationist, after a faithful life spent in the cause of Christ, passes beyond this life, he is reported not as having

---

[1] *The Vatican Revolution* (London: Macmillan, 1958), p. 120.

died but as having been "promoted to glory", as befits one of Christ's warriors.

Salvationist teaching on sanctity was distinctive from the first and has remained perhaps the most outstanding feature of Salvationist teaching today. The ideal of sanctity Booth set before his people had to be lived out, as well he knew, in the lowest levels of industrial society in late Victorian England.[1] I asked my friend Frederick Coutts, General of the Salvation Army, how he would describe the distinctiveness of Salvationist teaching on sanctity. General Coutts, in his reply, calls special attention to two points. He observes on the one hand that Booth inherited from Wesley "a horror of antinomianism".[2] He cites the resolution passed within the movement as early as 1873 that "no person shall be allowed to teach that . . . the moral law was abolished, and that if any person after being cautioned . . . continued to propagate this doctrine" such person must be forbidden to preach or speak. "To this formative period," writes General Coutts, ". . . belongs the introduction of the rule regarding total abstinence (from alcohol) and general non-conformity to 'the world'." On the other hand, the General wishes to stress that Booth's teaching was never "perfectionist". "He was too human a character to claim any such standard for himself or to impose such a yoke on others." He quotes the remark of Catherine Booth in one of her popular addresses in St. James's Hall, Piccadilly: "Neither is sanctification final growth. It does not imply final attainment. You must discriminate between purity and maturity. . . ." The General notes that in the current Salvation Army song book, 173 songs occur in the section entitled "The Life of Holiness", and out of these, 70 are by Salvationist writers. "The love of God shed abroad in the human heart was not regarded as an emotional experience, nor to be confused with such fringe experiences as speaking with tongues. 'Make character,' Catherine Booth would often say." Above all, the Salvationist ideal of sanctity excludes introverted piety. Booth's spirit is expressed in the following utterance: "If a brother or sister be naked, and destitute of daily food, and one of you say unto them, 'Depart in peace, be ye warmed and filled'; notwithstanding ye give them not those things which are needful to the body; what doth it profit?" Finally, there can be no "levels" of sanctity, according to typical Salvationist teaching. General Coutts quotes Catherine Booth: "I do not find two standards

[1] Booth published his influential book, *In Darkest England and the Way Out*, in 1890.
[2] The heresy that a Christian is not subject to the moral law because he is saved by grace and therefore can do whatever he pleases. [Ed.]

of Christian experience . . . at all. I do not believe God ever intended there should be a lower and a higher life . . . I believe that religion is all or nothing. God is either first, or He is nowhere with us at all." "God first" is indeed the battle cry of Salvationism. For the generality of mankind today it sets forth a fundamental idea enshrined in the Jesuit watchword *Ad majorem dei gloriam*: "To the greater glory of God."

The Pentecostal Movement

Out of an American holiness movement in the South and Middle West in the last few years of the nineteenth century, arose such bodies as the Pentecostal Holiness Church, pre-millenial in belief[1] and stressing (a) Wesley's doctrine of perfection and the personal sanctification of the believer, and (b) baptism in the Holy Spirit, accompanied by *glossolalia*, that is, "speaking with tongues". Pentecostalism appeared in Britain in September 1907, when a Methodist minister from Oslo, T. B. Barratt, who had contacts with Pentecostalism in the United States, was invited to conduct revival meetings at All Saints' Parish Church, Sunderland; but in 1925 and 1935 it received its greatest impetus through the preaching of the Jeffreys, three Welsh evangelists. The Elim Four Square Gospel Alliance had begun in Ireland under George Jeffreys in 1915.

Divine healing has always played an important role in Pentecostal practice. Speaking with tongues is expected to have beneficial results in health. The very gift of the Holy Spirit, it releases the healing forces within us. That sanctity has a healing aspect is, of course, widely recognised. The Very Reverend Lord MacLeod of Fuinary (George MacLeod) has for long made much of the notion of divine healing in the work of the Iona Community he founded, though to the best of my knowledge he has not encouraged *glossolalia* in the Pentecostal sense.

There are now in America various groups, some Methodist in origin, other Baptist, such as the Pentecostal Fire-Baptised Holiness Church and the Pentecostal Free-Will Baptists. The largest denomination deriving from that general American holiness movement is the Assemblies of God. This Church, founded at Hot Springs, Arkansas, April 2-12, 1914, now has about a million adherents, over eight thousand ordained clergymen, and a similar number of churches located in every State in the Union as well as in seventy-two other countries, including Britain, where it constitutes the largest Pentecostal denomination.

---

[1] That is, believing in the imminent return of Christ, to be followed by a thousand years of peace during which He will reign over the earth. [Ed.]

One of my former students, Dr. Gordon Fee, minister of one of the American churches and also a promising young New Testament scholar,[1] has kindly offered me his own observations, which he has first discussed at length with some of his colleagues, on the Pentecostal conception of holiness. Dr. Fee writes that "great emphasis is placed on individual religious experience . . . It is individual, hence there is little concern for social programs; it is religious, or 'spiritual' – which usually involves emotional manifestation; and it is an *experience* – everyone is expected to have a datable, usually emotional, experience of 'baptism in the Holy Spirit' . . . with its manifestation of *glossolalia* . . . Pentecostal sanctity has a profound awareness of the immediacy of God through the agency of the Spirit . . . If there is a distinctive type of personal holiness . . . it would have to be called 'joyous love'. My own relationship with Pentecostals, and that which I personally find attractive, is their infectious joy. They are reminiscent of Paul, whose legacy from a Roman prison was the Philippian paean of praise. This joy, the Pentecostal wants to be contagious. Therefore, he usually has a genuine concern for his neighbor. But this concern is almost always for the individual, seldom for the masses. . . ."

Dr. Fee, however, makes the sad observation that legalistic standards of conduct mar the ideal of sanctity in this denomination. He attributes this legalism to two factors. One is historic: it probably springs "directly from the Holiness movement within which Pentecostalism was born". The other is an inevitable perversion that arises from the way in which sanctity is conceived, for too often holiness "amounts to nothing more than conformity to sets of legal standards". The same perversion is well known, of course, in all traditions that make emotional experience a norm or calculus of sanctity. Dr. Fee notes the anomaly that people who put "such strong emphasis on the individual's relation to the Holy Spirit" should "so completely mistrust the Holy Spirit . . . by setting up all sorts of rigid rules for conduct in the matter of personal holiness".[2]

Underpinnings of personal holiness

What are the philosophical presuppositions of Christian holiness in all its modes and in all the richly variegated facets of its expression? Basically, the notion of holiness as developed in Christian thought and

---

[1] He has already published articles on Bodmer Papyrus II in *Novum Testamentum* and the *Journal of Biblical Literature*.
[2] One of the best available books on the subject is: John T. Nichol, *Pentecostalism*, New York: Harper and Row, 1966.

practice presupposes that man not only *does* good or evil acts; he *is* a good or evil man in the sense that whatever he is in the very root of his being, is capable of development into something that is good or evil in itself. What the man does is not, then, the reason for attributing sanctity or its absence to him; it is, rather, a token, an evidence, an expression, of a reality that lies within the man himself. "You shall be holy; for I the Lord your God am holy." (Lev. 19.2) The Christian Fathers, borrowing many ideas from Plato, Plotinus and the Stoics, specifically taught that man is in his essence a spiritual being; he is a *psyche*, a soul, and this soul may be healthy or diseased. The rash that may appear on a man's skin is not a measure of his sickness or his health. A singularly healthy man may look unsightly for a time on account of a black eye or a bruised nose, while a man riddled with a malignant disease may to all appearances look perfectly well. So the spiritual health or goodness of a man, whatever it is, must be determined, in the last resort, by what he is in his inmost being. In the long run the tree is indeed known by its fruits; but the absence of fruit does not necessarily mean that the tree is useless or diseased. The fructification process may be slow. As in biological life the swiftest maturation by no means necessarily results in the grandest achievements, so in the interior life the attainment of spiritual worth may be so slow as to exhaust the patience of some observers.

Such are the general underpinnings of the Christian doctrine of man and the Christian interpretation of his capacity for growth in worth, which are much modified, of course, in modern philosophical reflection on the Christian doctrine of man.

There is, however, a specific *theological* doctrine in Christianity, according to which the sanctification of the individual soul is accomplished through union with Christ in the Body that is His Church. As I have already noted, the heirs of the Reformation, no less than Christians in other traditions, recognise that tares (evil and hypocritical men and women) do exist in the Church alongside of the good wheat. Or we may say, in another classic metaphor, the Devil builds his chapel in the midst of God's Church. In terms of the New Testament "Body of Christ" figure we may perhaps say that cancerous cells mimic the healthy ones on which they are parasitic. Even so, one might object that what is difficult to understand is not the presence of diseased cells in the Body of Christ (Satan's vile functionaries who find Christ's Body their most profitable place of business); what astonishes and perplexes us is, rather, the vast area of benign tumour in the Body. By this I mean, of course, the presence of so many people in the Church who seem to be both useless and harmless, being neither actively healthy nor yet actively malignant. Unlike the evil men in the Church (whom the Reformation Fathers, in their robust sixteenth-century language, called Antichrist), these Laodiceans do not seem bent on destroying Christ's Church; yet unlike the saints they seem to do nothing for her and certainly fail to exhibit the life of Christ and the power of the Holy Spirit. Who are these benign tumours on the Body of Christ who are neither the offspring of the Devil nor the children of God? Christian theology, it would seem, ought to have more to say about them and a better explanation of their place in the scheme of things than any so far offered. This is certainly no place to embark upon so difficult an enquiry. I think we must carefully note, however, that in our age there is a particular need for an answer to that question, indeed for a treatment of it that would provide a full theological explanation to clarify a situation that many find at the best uninspiringly odd and at the worst, unbearably perplexing.

My chief purpose in mentioning it here is to draw attention to a derivative circumstance. While singling out saints would seem odd if it meant singling out healthy cells in the Body of Christ, when there were no others except for the malignant ones unsuccessfully attempting its destruction, it ceases to be odd when the Body of Christ seems to consist principally of vast areas of benign tumour. Then only, may we begin to speak as we do with delighted astonishment of discovering a saint in the Household of God. True, we similarly speak of heroes in a battle, without feeling we need expect every enlisted soldier to be of their number; but so arduous is the task of the Church Militant that unless it is a *corps d'élite*, an army in which heroism is normal, it cannot efficaciously fight the battles of the Lord. Worse still, these battles seem to many to be increasingly waged from outside the borders of the Visible Church, as though few of the children of God could any longer breathe within her. Such misgivings raise searching questions indeed, and cannot be indefinitely ignored in an age in which the Church feels a pressure towards an ecumenicity for long by many bitterly resisted. Much re-thinking must be done by theologians, and the fact and nature of Christian holiness must be increasingly the subject both of their thought and of the prayers of the faithful. Here is, indeed, perhaps, the most promising focus for an authentic ecumenicity that would be acceptable to the mind of God's people and attuned to the heart of the Mystical Body of Christ our Lord.

The more glaringly pagan undercurrents in the Christian heritage are generally held suspect among the heirs of the Genevan Reformation. For instance, von Hügel's descriptions of the psycho-physical feeling experienced by St. Catherine of Genoa (1447-1510) "of mostly interior, but later on also of exterior, warmth, indeed often an intense heat or burning . . . as though sunshine were bathing her within or with-out . . ."[1] do not tend to commend the saint to ears accustomed to a tradition of reticence. They suggest the "magical heat" that some ancient texts in Tantric yoga frankly specify as caused by "trans-mutation" of sexual energy. Professor Eliade has pointed out that the Sanskrit word *tapas*, now roughly translatable "the practice of asceti-cism", originally means simply "heat". As early as the Rig-Veda, however, which was committed to writing about the eighth century B.C., the practice of austerities was seen to be "heat-producing"; hence, presumably, the development of the secondary meaning of *tapas*.[2] The Reformed tradition derives great strength from its acute awareness of the reality of the gulf that lies between such phenomena as "heat magic" on the one hand and Christian sanctity on the other. Yet the fear of the pagan can also be a fatal weakness among the less sanctified of Geneva's heirs, for it springs from a dangerously simplicist psychology. Christian saints are no more afraid of the pagan underpinnings of the Christian notion of sanctity than one is afraid of a senile grandparent. Mature people are not afraid of the past. We fear the past only when we are immature enough to have reason to suspect that the past still holds us in its dread power. Forward-looking people love the past. Where there is hope there is history.

Not the least delightful discovery about genuine Christian holiness is surely the fact that, while it is essentially one, its manifestations are as varied as are the individuals who exhibit it. These saintly individuals are to be found in every branch of Christ's Church, whose structure is now labyrinthine. But how is the modern enquirer to carry out the biblical injunction to "believe not every spirit, but try the spirits whether they are of God: because many false prophets are gone out into the world"? (John 4.1). The New Testament writer of these words goes on to provide a criterion for testing: belief in the divinity of Christ. In the ancient Church a rule for determining Catholic orthodoxy was proposed, called later the Vincentian Rule: we are to believe that which

---

[1] Baron Friedrich von Hügel, *The Mystical Element of Religion* (2nd ed.; London: J. M. Dent and Sons, 1923), vol. I, p. 178.
[2] Mircea Eliade, *Myths, Dreams and Mysteries* (New York: Harper Torchbooks, 1967), pp. 92-95. This book is a translation of *Mythes, Rêves et Mystères*, Paris: Gallimard, 1957.

has been believed everywhere, always, and by all. In the complex world of today, such rules are not easy to follow. Moreover, while there have always been strange cults and seemingly weird religious groups, and there is certainly no lack of them today,[1] there are saintly characters in them too and notoriously no lack of very unsaintly ones in less heterodox quarters. Saints are found in the most unexpected places. How then shall a plain man tell whether a reputed saint be of God or of the Devil? Or, as many would prefer to put the question: how shall he know whether a man who *looks* holy *is* holy inside or vile? The teachings and practices of spiritualists, theosophists and other heirs of the Gnostic teachers who vexed the Church in early times continue to puzzle many. The complexity of the best modern scholarship that learned Christians have provided for the Church in our time seems sometimes to perplex more minds than it clarifies. How then are we to discern the true saint? And how shall we spot the fraud?

The little Quaker girl noticed that many ingredients are needed to make a saint, as many ingredients are needed to make a good cake. We have seen that there are many kinds of "cake" that are very good indeed. Moreover, good ingredients alone do not make a good cake. The baker must put into his cake more than flour and currants and the like. He must put into it diligence, skill, and a love of his work. Yet one thing is needful above all. Unless he can trust his source of supply he can never be sure that his cake is not poisoned. He cannot afford to eat his own cake if he lacks this confidence. If *he* cannot trust it, how can the dinner guests? If he can, why should not they? So when we see men and women so trustful of God's love and power that they feel they can *afford* to be courageously meek and quietly fearless before their fellow-men, even with the cards stacked against them, even indeed in the knowledge that the martyr's stake is being readied for them by the wicked, perhaps even within the Church itself, we can afford to feel confident that they are holy enough for us to admire, as Christ alone is holy enough for us to follow. Otherwise, I think we do well to wait before canonising them in our hearts. God's saints trust Him so profoundly that they can afford to pour themselves out unstintingly, as in the words of the prayer of St. Ignatius Loyola, "to toil, and not to seek for rest; to labour and to ask for no reward, save that of knowing that we do Thy will".

"The strong wine of religion is most plainly seen in the saints," notes a young American philosopher of religion. He goes on, however, to note

---

[1] See, for example: Marcus Bach, *Strange Sects and Curious Cults*, New York: Dodd, Mead 1961.

that even where the wine is "well watered, as in most lives that are not particularly religious, the meaning of religion does not have to be changed", for holiness provides "a standard that can measure both high degrees and low".[1] That holiness has this function makes it a most promising focus of mutual understanding and respect that can break down the inherited barriers that have already gravely undermined the efficacy of the Church as the special instrument of God. Yet we must remember, too, that nothing has so undermined the work of God in the Church as the presence in it of so many people who remain content to admire the saints from a "safe" distance without trying to follow Him who is the very spring of holiness.

If we have ever seen a saint at all, even for a brief moment, we know very well what a saint is and we truly want to pursue the path of holiness he has followed with such success. What, then, could make us fail, where he has succeeded, in that which is really the deepest desire of our hearts? One of the greatest of Christian thinkers, Søren Kierkegaard (1813-1855), provides a parable with which I shall conclude, as an awesome answer to that terrifying question. He asks us to suppose that the aim of the Christian life is to go to the North Pole, which in Kierkegaard's day seemed indeed a formidable enterprise, since at that time nobody had ever been there. Christians generally become convinced, however, that while going to the North Pole is a splendid ideal it is not a practical possibility. Nevertheless, one should not entirely abandon the notion on that account, they argue, because an ideal, however unattainable, ought to be pursued. So one Christian who lives in Copenhagen travels in comfort by steamship to London and back again, feeling that, though he did not reach the North Pole, he did try, and he even got some distance in the right direction, since London is north of Copenhagen. So even if another should take only a drive on Sunday afternoon in a park to the north of Copenhagen he is in the same case: he has not got to the North Pole, of course; yet he has gone in the right direction.

What terrible Christian satire! What a devastating indictment of those who are satisfied to be the benign tumour on the Body of Christ! To know what holiness is, means to know one ought to attain it. The rest is hard work, for as Zachary Boyd observed, our goal "is not winne with a wish". That work is immeasurably lightened, however, by the discovery that more people around us than we ever before noticed are

---

[1] Frederick Ferré, *Basic Modern Philosophy of Religion*. (New York: Charles Scribner's Sons, 1967), p. 71.

in the same predicament and share our infinite opportunity. Perhaps the most encouraging reflection of all is that if we are granted Christian sanctity we shall be more fully ourselves than ever before, for the saint is of all men the most thoroughly individualistic. No one else could possibly be like him. He is inimitable.

Holiness

in

The Catholic Tradition

by

Philip Caraman S.J.

Philip Caraman, S.J., F.R.S.L., M.A.(Oxon.), was born in London 1911. Educated at Stonyhurst and Oxford, he entered the Society of Jesus in 1930. At present he is Professor of Church History at the Westminster Diocescan Seminary at Ware, Hertfordshire. His books include *John Gerard, Henry Garnet, The Other Face, Angela Merici, C. C. Matindale, Norway* and he has edited *The Sermons of R. A. Knox* and *Saints and Ourselves* (3 volumes). His present essay was written in 1964.

HOLINESS is a state that commonly touches the experience of most men in a few encounters. Sometimes it is instantly recognised; at other times it is concealed under a disguise of ordinary behaviour. Its manifestation is infinitely varied. While it has certain constant features, it is not confined to any age or class. Usually it takes on the colour of a particular nationality, period or even climate; none has a prescriptive right to it. As many books have been written on the subject as on prayer, for it presents the perfect and only satisfying achievement in the life of the human soul.

Holiness, in this sense, might be defined as the perfect relationship between creature and Creator. For this reason it must interest all. Wherever it is met, in history or in life, it is acknowledged by Christian, heathen and atheist, but it cannot strictly be attributed to an unbeliever, no matter how exemplary he may be in his practice of the natural virtues, such as courtesy, morals or consideration for others. Socrates was perhaps a perfect gentleman; it is doubtful whether he can be described as a saint.

It can be said, without fear of contradiction, that the saint is truly great. While fulfilling the highest ideal given to man, he is at the same time a friend and an inspiration. In his individual way he tells us what we can achieve, whether we have one talent or ten, whether we live in comfort or poverty, sorrow or joy, in days of menace or of hope. He combines what might seem contradictories, weakness with strength, darkness with joy, self-denial with profound humanity and affection. Unlike most other persons of distinction, whether in literature, science or statesmanship, he remains contemporary, for he reveals the ever-lasting source of our happiness, the secret of how to turn the common into what is enduring and unique.

A saint himself and a beggar, Benedict Joseph Labre, wrote a prescription for sanctity: it contained a heart of fire for God, a heart of flesh for others and a heart of bronze for oneself.

Descriptions could be multiplied, but none that is exact mentions miracles or mystical phenomena: they may or may not accompany holiness, but they are no part of it, still less a measure of it; indeed they

G

are often found without it. Judas the Apostle, for instance, healed the lame and gave sight to the blind, but no writer of any creed has ever acclaimed him a saint.

The character of holiness

It is possible to have a unique assurance of holiness in the case of John the Baptist, since he was, so to speak, canonised by Christ himself (none greater than he was born of a woman), yet there is no record of any miraculous event or phenomenon in his life from the time he made his first appearance on the banks of the river Jordan not far from Jericho.

The character of his holiness is worth examining, at least briefly. At first glance he might appear to many an hirsute eccentric, even a fanatic, girt in goatskin, leaping among the rocks of the desert and living off honey and meal; yet in no other man are the constituents of holiness more sharply discernible. It is his inner disposition towards God, not his dress or diet, that holds the key to the subject of this symposium. His humility is manifest in his first encounter with Christ. Through his intense life of prayer he appreciated instantly that he was in the presence of a person with whom he could not endure comparison. "I should be baptised by you, not you by me"; he was not worthy to fasten the latch of his Master's sandal; all his own teaching was a feeble echo of his commanding authority. Here was no hollow protestation of humility, for on Christ's command, he obeyed and baptised him. To all who came down from Jerusalem to hear his preaching he had a word of counsel or comfort. The tax-gatherer should be just in his demands, the Roman soldier should protect, not harass, the down-trodden; the faithful must observe their religious fasts. Only for the Pharisee did he, like Christ, have bitter words. He was gentle, fearless in his denunciation, understanding of hardship, and affectionate. His Master paid him the compliment given to no other saint: he took his disciples and made them his own; he expanded his teaching, practised his baptism, borrowed phrases from his exhortations. And it was given also to the Baptist to formulate a charter of holiness valid for all time and unsurpassed in depth and succinctness. "He (Christ) must increase; I must decrease." The approach to holiness must be positive, the means clear – penance leading to the self-discipline demanded for companion-ship with Christ. The Baptist fits Benedict Labre's definition of a saint with a perfect exactness.

The Baptist's behaviour presents an example of total pliability to Christ's treatment: he lives only to be moulded to his likeness. He shows us also what lies in store for those who follow him. As soon as his Master begins his public ministry, he is left aside: henceforth he points away from himself towards him. When he is imprisoned for denouncing the morals of Herod's court, Christ does not intervene to rescue him: he is left forsaken and solitary to meet his brutal execution without complaint. In his last moments he foreshadows the desolate death of his Master on the Cross.

The Baptist is the last of the prophets and the greatest of the saints. In him the likeness to Christ is as near perfect as total correspondence with grace can make it. He has been given a part to play in a divine scheme and has kept to it heroically.

Yet neither the Baptist nor any other saint can be taken as a pattern for others. This is basic in any understanding of holiness, since every soul is an individual creation of God's unlike any of the millions made before it, and itself only one of infinite possibilities open to the Creator. Like the numberless celestial bodies of an undiscovered universe, each human soul has its unique purpose and place in God's design.

In other terms personal holiness is the fulfilment of this design. God and the individual are the two polar realities in the saint's life. It follows logically from God's infinite greatness that he can cherish, love and care for every soul as though none other existed. St. Paul understood this mystery, which became the inspiration of his apostolate. "Christ died *for me*," he wrote, meaning that Christ would have died for him alone. The very hairs of the individual's head are numbered like the grains of sand. To speak in human terms, God is capable of complete absorption in each and all of us. Humility, which all ascetical writers place at the foundation of sanctity, is only the acknowledgment of this total and inescapable dependence on God.

> Thee, God, I come from, to thee go,
> All day long I like fountain flow
> From thy hand out, swayed about
> Mote-like in thy mighty glow.[1]

Or, as the author of Wisdom writes, "If we sin we are thine, knowing Thy greatness: if we sin not, we are counted with Thee." (Wisdom 15.2) And again, in St. John's phrase, God is the Alpha and the Omega. The sadness of God, again to use human language, is the

---

[1] G. M. Hopkins, *Poems* (3rd edition), no 116. O.U.P.

sadness of an artist who sees his work mishandled, or rather, man-handled; and this also is the sadness of the saint as he looks out on a world that by rights belongs to God and by choice has rejected him.

There is an over-reaching divine scheme into which the holiness of each individual fits. St. John in the opening sentences of his Gospel expressed it in an exalted manner. Man's creation is given meaning in terms of the Trinity, his destiny by Christ's relationship to his Father: he is called to a divine sonship that entitles him to an unmerited share in God's life, the source of supreme love.

This is God's plan for him, but it cannot be imposed. It is a freely entered relationship since it is a relationship of love; it must involve deliberate choice. God's creature can make himself a child of the devil but he is given power to become a brother of Christ.

In whatever way various "schools" may express the ideal of sanctity, the differences are inessential. There can be no dispute on the end or the ideal. Whatever means are used, their purpose is to achieve a like-ness to Christ, to be moulded into an *alter Christus*. Emphasis and approach vary, but St. Paul's statement of the goal holds universally: "I live, no, not I, but Christ liveth in me."

The quality of love: human and divine

Holiness is achieved when, effortlessly, or rather by habit and grace acquired through effort, a man or woman thinks, acts, reacts, as Christ, revealing his charity in all circumstances to all God's creatures. Then he has not only the mind that is Christ's but his heart also, his courage, patience and endurance. Thus the saints in the calendar of the church, and outside the calendar, canonised and not, are truly "ten thousand" manifestations of the same Christ, since the saint:

> Acts in God's eye what in God's eye he is —
> Christ — for Christ plays in ten thousand places,
> Lovely in limbs, and lovely in eyes not his
> To the Father through the features of men's faces.[1]

In a familiar passage St. Paul lists the proliferations of the charity shown by the *alter Christus*. It matters little, indeed it is an accident of God's providence, whether the love that prompts all these virtues is actually felt or not, since it is situated in the will. Julian of Norwich, the English anchoress, speaks of an outstretching of the will to God; in reaching God the saint embraces all his interests and shares all his cares.

[1] G. M. Hopkins, "As kingfishers catch fire". *Poems* (3rd edition), no. 57.

For the true appreciation of holiness, this cannot be over-stressed. The love which in the Trinity passes between Father and Son and from eternity has begotten the Spirit of Love, is the same Love which encircles his creatures. Moreover, the love with which a saint loves God is the same love with which he loves his fellow men. The act is one act, enfolding two objects in a single embrace. When Francis of Assisi, in the valley below his native hill city, kissed a leper, he was given to understand that he was clasping none other than Christ himself. Catherine of Siena had an identical experience when she hugged a condemned criminal on the scaffold. To them and to all of us is offered the grace to appreciate this surpassing mystery of identification with Christ and to govern our lives by it.

To the extent a man acts on this principle, he will be judged. This is the refrain of Christ's discourse on the day of the last reckoning. Whether it is a cup of cold water offered to a parched traveller, or a visit to an imprisoned criminal, the act will count as a kindness to Christ himself. "As often as you did it to the least of these, you did it to me": not *as if* to me, but to me. Through the redemptive act of Christ the identification is made perfect.

It was left to St. John, at the close of his life, to reiterate in a dozen different ways this key mystery. God is near to us in all our neighbours; a husband is as closely one with his wife as Christ with his Church. Here is the wisdom of God, simple and luminous, reserved to those who, irrespective of age, are as children in their approach to him. It eludes the sophisticated. It is an inexhaustible mystery to all true mystics.

There can never be anything selfish in the pursuit of holiness, whether in the cloister or out of it, in marriage or in the single state. Although the strictly cloistered monk is segregated from the world, his prayer and suffering is for its sanctification as well as his own. God was ready to spare an entire people for a single just man; the petitions of the saint and his sacrifices are powerful before God, just as his death is precious in his sight. However sanctity is measured, it is not measured by output of work; there is nothing sanctifying in sheer toil:

> the vulgar mass . . .
> Things done, that took the eye and had
> the price.[1]

Only the inspiration of love gives work dignity and value before God, and only as an expression of love does it count for anything in his eyes.

[1] Robert Browning, "Rabbi Ben Ezra" (Penguin Selection), p. 263.

One act of un-selfregarding love of God can be more effective for the salvation of the world than a thousand deeds done without it.

For this reason the Church, from the beginning of her history, has set great store on the contemplative life and has fostered the vocation of the enclosed Christian, dedicated to the pursuit of intimacy with God. The vast number of religious Orders and Congregations, both of men and women, in the Catholic Church, and the varieties of western as well as eastern monasticism, present in differing blends a life of prayer and activity, but in the case of all, work is the overflowing of the hidden spirit of love. Often, after the passing of a crisis in the Church's history, the purpose of a religious Order has become redundant, and the Order itself extinct. None has a divine guarantee of permanency or is essential to the Church; only the contemplative life, in some form or other, is indispensable to her well-being.

"Love is but the infancy of true charity," wrote an English poet and martyr, Robert Southwell. He was using the word love in the sense it carried among Elizabethan gallants, who praised it in stylised poems written in the stiff framework of new and experimental rhythms. Already in his day it was a debased coinage exchanged in much the same manner as today. At best it meant a deep and passionate attachment, a blind emotion, which, compared with "true charity", was like a helpless and inarticulate infant. The source of both was the same, but Christ's love was manly, the other puerile. Augustine passed from the first to the second and his appreciation of the difference inspired his *Confessions*. Less well known is the relationship between them worked out meditatively by the same Elizabethan writer: love that fails to rise from the creature to the Creator is destined never to satisfy.

> If I love a creature, it cannot know how much nor in what manner my love is: but if I love God, he knoweth better the love of my heart than myself.
> If I love a creature, I find it not at all times, nor as often as I would, and I cannot speak to it as often as I desire and as need requireth, neither doth it hearken to my words as I wish: but if I love God, I have him at all times with me: I may speak to him as often as I please, and at all times he hearkeneth to my words, yea and to the desires of my heart.
> If I love a creature, oftentimes I have care of it: but if I love God, he hath care over me.

If I love creatures, I know not their secrets: but if I love God, he openeth often to me the truth of all hidden and secret things.

If I love a creature, it yieldeth not my heart's desire: but if I love God he will give me wholly all my desires.[1]

In the Christian teaching this distinction is vital. At the same time it is untruthful to represent the love of the Creator as incompatible with love of the creature: the creature is loved with greater understanding the more it is seen as a reflection of the Creator. The saint is not a person who makes himself less human in order to become more divine. His love of others is constant because it does not depend on mercurial affection or favours. He is close to God and therefore realistic. The springs of his love never dry up: it is reliable because it is altruistic and not measured by emotion; its bearings are taken on an unchanging God.

The happiness of the saints

This is the secret of the saints' happiness; and it can be said that only the saint experiences happiness in all circumstances. Also happiness is a characteristic of all saints, both in life and in death. The sad saint, said Francis de Sales in a much quoted phrase, is a sad sort of saint. The priest or nun who has an authentic calling is not lastingly affected by gloom or depression. Even the sense of humour the saints possess is enhanced by grace. Many, such as Philip Neri, were incurable jokers and kept their childlike charm unspoilt. Francis of Assisi manifestly took great pleasure from God's animal creation: he was conscious all the time of the concern of God for all that came from his hands. The joy he always manifested makes him attractive to Christian and pagan alike. While it is incorrect to claim that saints alone are true lovers, they are the best guides to the security of unchanging love.

Diversity of holiness

No particular way of life is needed for holiness. Men and women of every class and profession, every level of education, employment, age, intelligence, circumstance, upbringing and environment are found in the Roman martyrology. Some would seem to have made an uninterrupted spiritual progress from their early childhood; others, like Paul,

[1] For a fuller text, see *The Other Face* (ed. Philip Caraman), Longmans, pp. 179-180.

only after an abrupt divine intervention; others still, like Camillus de Lellis, after several lapses and fresh beginnings. They all have their place in the calendar, beggars, kings, theologians, peasants, sick and ailing, serf and free. "Be ye perfect as your heavenly Father is perfect" is a command given to every adopted son of God and it holds without exception for all times, places and people wherever the gospel is preached.

As St. Thomas Aquinas insists,[1] nothing should be discarded in a Christian's friendship with God: "all his acts should go to him, all his loves be brought into the love of God, every deed and word based on it. Such is the perfect mode of charity, to which all are bound by necessity of precept." Today, as in the past, martyrs and confessors are drawn from every country: natives of Uganda and Japan, Spain, England, Portugal, France and Peru. At periods of crisis in the Church's history there appear to have been more recognisable saints than in times of quiet. When Ignatius of Loyola first visited Rome at Easter, 1523, there could be found in Europe at least seven founders of Religious Orders later canonised by the Church, not to mention many saintly bishops, priests and nuns.

Partnership with God

In the partnership that constitutes holiness God assumes the controlling role: He is the head, as Christ is head of the Church. The soul is fashioned to God's likeness, not *vice versa*, and the force that establishes this likeness works with a power that can hardly be compared with the effort of the individual. Man must cooperate; there must be, not only willingness on his part, but positive choice and sustained determination, yet his effort is little more than a token of his desires. Indeed the Christian soul is not unlike the infant who attempts to push a toy wheelbarrow: he stumbles again and again until God, coming from behind him, takes hold of the shafts and walks with him. Only the saint who knows what God has done for him can ascribe nothing to himself. To others it often seems that he speaks of himself in terms of excessive self-disparagement. It strikes the uninitiated as hyperbole that a man of manifest innocence should describe himself as a great sinner deserving God's worst punishments; yet to the saint there is nothing untruthful or exaggerated in this. His language is a gauge of his closeness to God, against whom all his actions are measured. He is so aware of his

---

[1] *De Perfectione Vitae Spiritualis*, 5.

indebtedness that any trivial deviation from unselfish love is seen as the darkest ingratitude. He walks with God, converses with him, receives his favours in prayer, his guidance is by the illumination of his understanding. Because his standards are not of this world, they are incomprehensible to other men. In the phrase of a priest poet, his days are dressed to a "dexterous and starlight order" which is a prevision of heavenly truth.

Human temperament and talents

The key to God's assessment of the saints is given in the parable of the talents. To some, one talent is given, to others three, five or ten. If the talents are taken to include not only God's gifts of mind, heart, soul and body, but also disposition, inherited fears, opportunities of education and upbringing, and even psychological deviations, it is possible to form a tentative but necessarily inexact estimate of the response of the soul to grace. It is a hoary maxim that grace does not eliminate nature; it enhances and perfects it. The same strength of will that leads to outbursts of rage is nursed in the saints to become a firm cleaving to God. Their impatience, short temper, sharpness of speech, the inclination to idleness or indulgence, are not killed but doctored to a divine end. It is a false hagiography that sets the saint in a category unattainable by ordinary individuals: the truthful hagiographer shows how the human has been made perfect by the divine; he does not omit the involuntary flaws found always alongside heroic virtue.

Although, as was pointed out earlier, the precept of holiness excludes none, its application differs with the individual. The saintliness of a monk is not that of a missionary; that of a married woman is not the same as a nun's. In marriage, for instance, husband and wife seek in partnership the perfection proper to their state. What is the interest of one becomes the concern of both; and in loving each other they grow in their love of God; their task is ever to give, according to a statement of Our Lord that is recorded outside the gospels: "It is more blessed to give than to receive." (Acts 20.35) As with all other Christians, their love is a love that springs from the Holy Trinity, a mystery depicted by mediaeval artists in a composition that sets out the motive of all true self-offering: the Holy Spirit as a dove hovering over the head of the bearded Father, who holds out his hands in the gesture of giving his only Son to the world. In the Christian concept of marriage neither happiness nor sanctity is attainable without a total self-giving that leads ultimately to identification. A man finds his life only when he loses it, receives everything when he gives all away. What he gives he receives back, not merely in measure abundant and overflowing, but in a degree infinitely enhanced by grace. Daily the saint experiences the hundred-fold promised by Christ to those who renounce all to follow him.

The true nature of love

All love is a divine gift; there is none more excellent. The celibate or cloistered saints of the Church discover a more embracing love than that expressed in marriage. No outsider can begin to comprehend a saint if he starts from the assumption that natural and human love must be stifled before the first steps are taken towards sanctity. Saints are the greatest lovers God has made. As God so loved the world that he gave it his Son, the saint so loves God that he gives himself, not to another person but to the world. Loving and life-giving are inextricably interwoven. St. John the Evangelist never writes of the one without mentioning the other. Artificial separation brings disaster. There is passion, emotion, ecstasy and unspeakable satisfaction in what, to use a modern phrase, can be called the love-life of a saint. He knows that his love is reproductive in a plane higher than the physical. It is not a question of substitution, not even of sublimation, but of a love that not even those who have experienced it can adequately describe. Everything is fuel for it; no alteration of circumstances can diminish it; its nature is as enduring and its bounds as limitless as God who is its object.

It was the love Christ showed for others that attracted disciples to him. In their faltering way they sought to become like him and to do as he did. With difficulty he taught them that this likeness could be achieved only through suffering: here was the stumbling-block for them as it is for us. The daily happiness of the disciples of Christ comes through the daily carrying of the cross: exaltation cannot be had except by drinking the cup that he himself drank. The image of the Master must be reproduced through a crucifixion.

This is not something sought for itself, but for its divinising action. After Peter had protested his love three times, Christ foretold his death: " 'When you were young, you fastened your belt about you and walked where you chose; but when you are old, you will stretch out your arms, and a stranger will bind you fast and carry you where you have no wish to go.' He said this to indicate the manner of death by which Peter was to glorify God. Then he added, 'Follow me'." (John, 21.18-19)

Suffering and asceticism

Only the desire for identification with Christ gives meaning to the desire for suffering. Suffer or die, was the cry of St. Teresa of Avila, who saw in suffering shared with Christ the surest token of his love, the guarantee of her closeness to him who undertakes to chastise every child he receives. So also it is the unmistakable mark of the favoured apostle: the redemptive mission of Christ can be continued only by men and women prepared to share in the mystery by which the world was won back to God.

Readiness to suffer for a person or cause is, moreover, the test of genuine attachment. If love is proved by deed more than by speech, it is sifted by suffering: the dross falls away, and what remains is purified by fire. Purgation is as essential for the vision of God in the next life as suffering for companionship with him in this. God's purity is such that it can endure no attachment that conflicts with the possession of him. He is a jealous God whom the Christian serves and his name must be engraven on his heart.

For every individual, God reserves his suffering until he is spiritually mature. As St. Paul says, God does not permit a soul to be tried beyond its strength but with the trial brings also relief. The worst-recorded temptations against chastity were experienced by St. Anthony, the first hermit, after years in the desert where he had been in hourly communication with God. His rejection of them strengthened his love, as it does in the instance of every soul. It is the same temptation that makes the saint and the sinner.

Self-inflicted suffering, whatever name it goes by — penance, mortification, self-denial or abnegation — has value only as a preparation of the soul to meet trial. It is an asceticism essential for the Christian athlete, as St. Paul shows in his epistle to the Corinthians (1 Cor. 9.24-27) and the Church reiterates in her directives on penance. A child, untutored in self-restraint, is incapable as an adult of unselfish loving; the Christian is taught to bring his instincts into subjection that he may receive and retain the more precious love of God.

Asceticism is less assistance towards holiness than the patient acceptance of the suffering which God designs for each as his share of his cup. In human terms, Christ himself was more ready to redeem the world in any way rather than in the way appointed by his Father. The supreme utterance of his infinite holiness is his agonised prayer, "Let this cup pass from me; yet not my will but thine be done." Likewise when a Christian prays, "Thy will be done", he is praying for nothing other than his individual sanctification. The climax of his love comes with the elimination of all differences between 'thou' and 'I'. The sufferings of God become his. Disgrace, loss of good name among men, calumny and rejection are all contained in the cup set before those who are ready to go Christ's way. Poverty or, in its positive aspect, dependence on God, is another ingredient of the same grace; still more, failure and frustration. Although in the estimate of historians many saints, through the reforms they initiated or the religious families they founded, made a more lasting impression on the world than emperors, kings or governments, their own achievement was hidden from them in their day; only their sinfulness and the shoddiness of their work was at all apparent to their own eyes. This is inevitable if the pattern of Christ's life is to be repeated in his apostles. The seed must die. At the moment of Christ's own death on the Cross, only Mary and a few women, only John among the apostles, remained by him from the thousands that had listened to his teaching and benefited by his works. The saint triumphs after his death, as Christ did after Calvary. A special enlightenment is needed before a Christian can say, "I have fought the good fight, I have kept the faith. Now an imperishable crown of glory is prepared for me." It comes to few; most must beg God to be merciful to his poor servant, and then commend their soul to his hands.

Some holy men in their dying moments have feared abandonment by God because their passage to him has been painless. God's treatment of each of his saints is different. Although suffering is the lot of all, no two suffer in the same manner. There is a mystery in God's individual handling of every soul he has made, a private and peculiar mystery that draws together God and his creature, a secret as closely guarded as the most intimate passages of love between wife and husband. No stranger can penetrate it. As man cannot begin to comprehend God's nature, he cannot enter into the depth of his individual dealing with the soul. We hold fast to the Creed as the formulation of the mysteries revealed to us through Christ; there are other mysteries that will be revealed only when we shake off the restrictions of this flesh. With the individual it is the same. The gospels give indications of the treatment we are to expect from God's hands, but they contain only incomplete clues to this private mystery that will be fully unfolded at the hour God and the soul meet face to face.

However, God's general purpose in permitting his saints to suffer

even death for his sake is perhaps best epitomised in a few sentences of
Robert Southwell, who compares the Father to a rag-picker. "And as
a paperer of old rotten shreds," he writes,[1] "oftentimes gathered out of
unclean dunghills, by his industry maketh so fine white and clean paper
that it is apt to receive any curious drawing, painting or limning: so
our scattered parts ... cast into dunghills, he will restore to such purity
of perfection that they shall be more capable of His glorious ornaments
than they were before."

Here lies the cause for joy, indeed for joking. Walking over London
Bridge on an autumn afternoon in 1591 in company with a nobleman,
Southwell laughed when he saw the heads of martyrs fastened on the
point of pikes: "his face lit up with an extraordinary gaiety (his friend
reported) and he said, 'O, my Lord, if God grants it, you will see *my*
head sometime on one of those pikes.' "[2]

Martyrdom

From the time of St. Andrew the Apostle, who gave an ecstatic
embrace to the Cross, through Ignatius of Antioch, impatient to reach
Rome to be eaten there by lions, to the butcher's wife of York, Margaret
Clitheroe, martyrdom has been considered by the Christian the highest
privilege God can offer him, for it is an indisputable proof of His love
and the attainment in death of a more complete likeness to Him.

It must not be thought that there is anything fanatical in the lives of
martyrs. Their death is a privilege they would be foolhardy to court;
they know that their strength to endure it comes not from themselves
but from God. Felicity, the African matron, speaks for them all. She
was eight months with child. As she waited its birth in her cell, she
came to be "oppressed with her travail", the *Acta* tell us,[3] "and made
complaint". Then one of the servants of the doorkeeper said to her,
"Thou that thus maketh complaint now, what wilt thou do when
thou art thrown to the beasts, which thou didst contemn when thou
wouldst not sacrifice?" She answered, "I myself now suffer that which
I now suffer, but there another shall be in me who shall suffer for me,
because I am to suffer for him."

Margaret Clitheroe used similar phrases. Of course, she feared death,
but at the same time she was confident that the courage she needed

[1] *Epistle of Comfort* (1587), 203-204.
[2] C. Devlin, Robert Southwell, 235. Sidgwick and Jackson, 1967.
[3] *The Passion of SS. Perpetua and Felicity.* (trans. W. H. Shewring) Sheed and Ward, 1931,
36.

would certainly be given from God, since it was he who had destined her for this trial of her love. Her cause, as she said, was "God's quarrel", and she added: "I confess death is fearful and flesh frail, yet I mind by God's assistance to spend my blood for my faith, as willingly as ever I put my paps to my children's mouths."[1]

Moreover, the saying of Tertullian that the blood of the martyrs is the seed of Christians has proved true in all periods of history. The faith they died for rather than deny has survived or revived in all countries where persecution sought to extinguish it. And the reverse is sadly true: today the Christain faith has only a small foothold in countries where none was found to surrender his life rather than compromise his conscience. Rome, the principal arena of the early martyrs, later became the mistress of western Christendom.

Nothing could be more remote from the heart of any English Catholic than the desire to rekindle ancient animosities by seeking the full honours of canonisation for those men and women, representative of all ranks and classes of society, who gave their lives rather than renounce what they held to be the ancient faith of their countrymen. They were victims of a totalitarian monarchy; the death they suffered was the penalty, not of heresy, but of high treason; they knew that no effort of theirs counted for anything in the struggle to win others to their belief, that only God's grace could bring that about. Yet if they were to stay true to their conscience, there was no choice before them. Heroism was commanded of them by him who alone can command it and can give also the needed grace with the command. "So the faith was planted, so it shall be restored" was their settled assurance.

At a later day and hour when the same integrity is required in different and severer trials their example will be a source of strength to their fellow believers; canonisation will spotlight their lives. Whatever has been written in praise of the ancient martyrs, can be written of them – I use the word in the strict sense the Church gives it. More broadly, and etymologically, a martyr is any person who in his death gives witness to his belief; and for this he is always to be honoured. But, obviously, the Church can be concerned only with those of her children who gave this ultimate witness to the beliefs she maintains. Archbishop Laud can rightly be held a martyr of Anglican belief, Charles I of the principle of monarchy: none would wish to acclaim them as martyrs of the Catholic Church. It is logical that they should be given the title by the communions in which they bore witness.

[1] Cf. *The Other Face*, 229.

Spiritual phenomena

An essay on holiness must contain some notice of the phenomena that sometimes accompany it: ecstasy, the stigmata, rapture, levitation, and the rest. As far as is known, many of the greatest saints never experienced any charismata. St. Paul was rapt to the third heaven, transported out of his physical senses, heard voices and was shown a vision which even he was incapable of describing (2 Corinthians 12.1-5). John in his cave above the bay at Patmos was granted pictorial visions in a panoramic series. But while the saint, particularly the woman saint, is often a visionary, the converse does not hold. John and Paul put the essence of holiness in the love of God. Both recognised also that the territory of such experiences was commonly disputed between God and the devil.

To work miracles, to speak in prophecy, to receive heavenly visitations are all unavailing without charity. In every age persons of all religions and of none have in different ways sought direct communication with God. The vast majority of claims to have achieved it can be rejected as spurious. Today the means used to induce states of ecstasy or mental transport are often utterly repulsive; in some instances a preliminary condition of mental excitement is deliberately created for this end: the result is frenzy, partial derangement or worse. Indeed it is wrong to seek such direct contact with God unless it is gratuitously granted, just as it is wrong to pry by dubious and nerve-wrecking methods into the secrets of the after-life.

In her treatment of all the physical phenomena of mysticism, whether in saints or others, the Church assesses each case on its presentation. She acknowledges that they can be genuine graces of God; sometimes, as in the case of Bernadette's visions at Lourdes, she gives them her blessings without necessarily setting her seal either on the occurrence or the accompanying locutions. Always her office is to reject errors and counterfeits, to sift evidence and insist on the essential requirements of holiness. Even when she canonises one of her children who has been specially favoured by visitations or voices from heaven she does not warrant their truthfulness.

Three examples of holiness

The well-known instance of Padre Pio has received much publicity in the post-war years. Here was a priest apparently bearing the stigmata or the physical impression on his body of the wounds suffered by Christ in his passion. Should the phenomenon be scientifically established (and it may well be) it has special interest. It would become the first known case of the stigmata in a man since it was given to Francis of Assisi, and the first ever in a priest.[1] The visitor to his convent on the mountain site above Mafredonia was certain to be impressed, as he served the Friar's Mass, by his rapturous concentration on the sacrifice, but was more impressed, I think, by the sight of the shrewd peasant priest seated in the open confessional in the sacristy, as his penitents from all parts of Italy and from all classes of society, knelt patiently waiting their turn to unburden their sins to him. Here was an unmistakable and manifest likeness to Christ to whom all who were in trouble came for divine comfort.

It is reported of Padre Pio that before his stigmata became visible he endured for a number of years the pain of invisible wounds. There have been men and women in England and elsewhere who have attracted in their time passing notice by the manifestation of similar phenomena, but what in all cases induces conviction is the humility and obedience of the sufferer.

Interesting but scarcely known even among Catholics is the strange phenomenon experienced by an Elizabethan priest, Arthur Bryant, in the year 1581, as he lay stretched on the rack in the Tower vaults some days before his execution at Tyburn. The account of it is written by himself. Like all genuine mystics, he had difficulty in framing words to explain what had passed. It is uncertain how a mystical theologian would classify the occurrence, but it is worth giving his own narrative: "Whether what I am relating be miraculous or no (he wrote), God knoweth but true it is, and therefore my conscience is a witness before God. And this I say, that in the end of the torture, though my hands and my feet were violently racked . . . yet, notwithstanding, I was without sense and feeling well nigh of all grief and pain; and not only so, but as it were comforted, eased and refreshed of the grief of past torture. . . . In the meantime (while waiting further torture the following day), I did muse and meditate upon the most bitter passion of our Saviour, and how full of innumerable pains it was. And whilst I was thus occupied methought that my left hand was wounded in the palm, and that I felt blood run out. But in very deed there was no such thing, nor any other pain than that which seemed to be in my hand."[2]

Nevertheless is is not for this experience that Father Bryant is

[1] St. Francis was ordained deacon, but he did not receive the priesthood.
[2] Cf. *The Other Face*, 243.

venerated as a saint, but for his death in defence of the faith without which he was unable and unwilling to live.

Apart from Padre Pio, who may in time be canonised, a German Jesuit priest, Rupert Mayer, gave me a strong impression of sanctity at my meeting with him. He had been a chaplain in the First World War, won the Iron Cross for his chivalry in ministering to the wounded in the trenches, and died in a prison camp during the Second World War. There was nothing charismatic in his spiritual life, but he had abundant and controlled charity. His features were rugged and handsome, his face heavily lined; his eyes possessed a disconcerting penetration. He spoke softly, his courtesy was unassumingly natural, his expression calm but indicative of continuous suffering, both physical (for he was lame) and spiritual (for he fought a lonely battle against evil). Unmistakably his friends were conscious of being confronted with a saint. At the height of Nazi power he preached bravely against the irreligion of the regime; he refused to be silenced, returning always to the defence of the conscientious rights of Catholic, Lutheran and Jew. When Hitler, whom he had known as a youthful private and an underground agitator, sent him a telegram of congratulation on his priestly jubilee, he tore up the paper in the pulpit before his congregation. With Pastor Niemöller, he became a symbol of resistance to a resurgent barbarism. Fearlessly he condemned blasphemous cartoons — it was the time German bookshops displayed prints depicting the Nazi Führer standing on a wooden table in a Munich beer cellar addressing his spell-bound disciples, with the caption below, *am Anfang war das Wort*, "In the beginning was the Word". Wherever he proposed to preach, though no public notice was given, hundreds were turned away from the crowded church. In and out of concentration camps this was his life for more than ten years. Today he is buried in the Burgersall Kirche in Munich. The stream of pilgrims there is incessant from morning till night.

Life in the spirit

Beneath the surface manifestation of all holiness lies the life of the spirit that is the possession of all who are at peace with God. It is called variously the divine or supernatural life or, simply, grace. It is the essence of our union with God, our claim to membership of his family, the pledge of our salvation, the deed that entitles us to call God our

H

Father. This is the life Christ came on earth to give: not simply a fuller human life, but one as distinct in kind from the rational life as the animal life is from the vegetative. It is as real as it is hidden; it has its beginnings in baptism, its full development in confirmation, its food in the Eucharist, its medicine in the sacrament of penance; it gives marriage a supernatural destiny and ministers spiritual strength to its partners. The stigmata can be considered an external manifestation of interior likeness to the suffering Christ. There is also among the established phenomena of mysticism a condition known as luminosity by which the face or limbs are lit with a more than human resplendence. This can be taken as an exceptional break-through of the interior life into the world of sense. There is only one instance of the phenomenon that is authentic beyond cavil, the transfiguration, as it is called, of Christ on the summit of Thabor. His purpose then was to re-enforce the faith of the Apostles who were shortly to witness his humiliation on the Cross. Christ's body became luminous and translucent; the three witnesses were blinded by the light that shone from him and realised fully, perhaps for the first time, that the human cloak of common man concealed in their Master this divine life which he came to offer all who would accept it.

This was a fleeting manifestation of Christ's holiness, not a proof of it, nor indeed any integral part. The true life of all saints is within. There are, in the history of the Church, countless uncanonised visionaries and ecstatics. No number or intensity of uncommon experiences is necessarily relevant to sanctity. It is other standards the Church uses when she is asked by her people to examine and give verdict on their holiness.

What are these standards? Whom does the Church declare saints? And by what process does she form her judgement?

The canonisation and veneration of saints

In the briefest account of canonisation it must be made plain that those who are declared saints by the Church are only a few among an unnumbered crowd who from accident of personal or national history, or lack of evidence or interest, have never been canonised or indeed are likely to be. Not even the Roman martyrology is a definitive catalogue; outside it there is a vast assembly of saints, men and women, unknown, unnamed and unrecorded on earth. Before God their merits are as great as others whose lives have been re-written many times to meet the fashion of succeeding generations. The Church was alert to this in her earliest years and among her most ancient feasts is that of All Saints, on which day all her children in heaven are namelessly invoked and commemorated. Their praises are sung in the *Te Deum*.

The act of canonisation in no way enhances the merits of a great servant of God. It is not for his own sake that a saint is so honoured — no act of any person or body on earth can alter, increase or diminish his inalienable happiness with God. By canonisation he is, as it were, elevated to a position among men from which his example can radiate over a wider area and at the same time show forth the power of God's grace over evil. God gains a kind of accidental glory from the saintliness of his children: their triumph is his achievement. As St. Leo the Great writes, men "glory in God, who is marvellous in his saints, whom he has raised for our protection and example".[1] Often it happens that the popular veneration of a saint wanes with the passing urgency of his example. Some, like the Magdalen, have a perennial lesson; others, a transitory message; some meet national needs, others local, a few universal. Occasionally it is the artist who fosters devotion. Historians have maintained that the popularity of St. Sebastian in the Middle Ages was due to the opportunity his story gave religious painters of portraying the naked human frame. Less explicably, certain saints, like Jude the Apostle, achieve a sudden widespread fame. St. Joseph, to whom no church was dedicated before the sixteenth century, has become internationally venerated in modern times.

During the first centuries of the Church, few were called saints except the martyrs. There could be no doubt about the heroism of their virtue which then, and since then, has been the basic requirement for canonisation: all could have saved themselves from the rack, sword or lions by the simple act of offering incense before the likeness of the reigning Emperor. Because the Christian community believed intensely in the ultimate resurrection of the body, the bones of these men were venerated, Mass was offered at their tomb, the day of their passion commemorated and in the liturgy their names recalled along with the Apostles of Christ. It was the excellence of their example that gave the martyrs priority of veneration and of merit among the saints. Once the fact and cause of their martyrdom was established, they were held worthy of honour, some in Rome, others in Africa, Gaul or the east. In the Roman Canon of the Mass their names were remembered and their heavenly intercession invoked.

[1] St. Leo, "Sermon for the Feast of St. Laurence".

The position of the saint in the liturgy of the Church was established in the era of the first martyrs. The veneration they received was strictly controlled. Dying as they did for their belief in one God, there was never danger that they might be given any form of worship due exclusively to him; nowhere in Christian writing is there any hint of the saints replacing the Greek or Roman deities: emphatically they were men of flesh and blood, heroes who gave a supreme example to their brethren striving to serve the same God. Their lives had merit before him and their prayers intercessory power. No divine attributes were ascribed to them nor miracles either, but their aid was sought with the certainty that their lives were united to God, just as in their lifetime the prayers of any holy man or woman had always been particularly treasured. In the litanies of the saints only God was asked for mercy; the saints were then called upon to intercede before God for the living; no incense or sacrifice was offered them. It was permitted to adorn a church or house with their likeness or ikon, but this was a device to recall the presence of persons dear both to them and God. Mementoes in the form of relics were kept, but this was a practice already customary among families in all countries both in Roman and earlier times.

Only after the close of the last Roman persecutions were men and women other than martyrs declared saints. In the primitive sense of the word a confessor was a Christian who gave witness to his faith by imprisonment or loss of possessions without undergoing actual martyrdom. He was a martyr by desire though not in deed, a martyr, so to speak, of the second degree. Many Church historians have seen in the eremitical movement (its beginnings coincided with the end of the persecution) a desire to find a substitute for martyrdom. The language of the first hermits is full of images drawn from their sufferings. In the teaching of Cassian the ideal perfection is pursued by mortification of the body that makes possible a vivification of the spirit by God: obedience is stressed in imitation of the obedience of Christ to His Father and of the martyr to the voice of his conscience. Like the martyr, the monk is led where he does not choose to go. St. Paul, the first hermit, and St. Anthony, the first founder of a community of hermits, were, after their death, venerated in much the same manner as the martyrs of an earlier century. Popular cult gave them a place in heaven as secondary heroes, and the Church graded them below the martyrs in her calendar. There followed the holy virgins and, after them, widows like Monica. By accident, perhaps, rather than for canonical reasons, there was lacking a category of married persons who had predeceased their partner.

Before the centralisation of the Church's government by Pope Hildebrand in the eleventh century very little effective control was exercised by Rome over the declaration of saints. Previously, intermittent and for the most part unsuccessful efforts had been made to investigate the virtue of holy persons already acclaimed saints in their native city, diocese or country: the prefix was attached to their names without the endorsement of the Church; often the memory of them — men like St. Ives and the saints that have given their name to Cornish villages — died within a generation: in their case only an embryonic process of canonisation was instituted, perhaps none at all. Sages, hermits, visionaries and prophets, venerated in their lifetime, were popularly hailed as saints; many persons of eminence or power, like Olaf, Charlemagne, Alfred and Knut were given the title by their own or succeeding generations but were never formally canonised. The first formal process, as it is called, or examination of an English saint was instituted in the case of Edward the Confessor. In the volumes of the Rolls Series can be found the material of the first investigation instituted with the purpose of canonisation. There is, first, the *vita* or life, then the record of alleged miracles worked by God through his intercession, and, finally, the testimony of the witnesses to his virtue. Apart from certain elaborations the lines of enquiry are substantially unaltered today. The volumes dealing with Thomas Becket in the next century, though more detailed, are similar in plan.[1] Later the writings of the saint were subjected to examination for orthodoxy; later still, a distinction was made between processes that involved contemporary witnesses and others that were purely historical. Into this second class would fall the twentieth-century process on St. Albert the Great, the teacher of Aquinas, who was canonised when he was proclaimed a Doctor of the Church by Pius XI in December 1931.

The last English confessor to be declared saint was Thomas Canteloupe, Bishop of Hereford, who died in 1282 and was canonised by John XXII in 1320. At that time many processes had already been instituted into the lives of other saintly English monks, anchoresses and bishops, but most of them were held up by the Hundred Years War, later still by the Reformation; few were ever resumed. In this category

[1] For Edward the Confessor see the Rolls Series, volumes 3 and 6, for Thomas Becket, volumes 65, 67, 73.

falls the process on King Henry VI.[1] The first enquiries are extant, and
it is possible, though unlikely, that his cause will be resumed in modern
times. The canonisation of Jeane D'Arc could be taken as a precedent
for such a course.

Throughout the Middle Ages the Popes attempted both to tighten
their control over the canonisation of saints and at the same time to
regulate the honours paid to them. An intermediate stage to full
canonisation was instituted when, before the completion of the process,
a servant of God was declared "blessed". Beatification, as it was called,
did not commit the Church to an incontrovertible statement on heroic
virtues; very limited honours were allowed the *beatus*; no church could
be dedicated in his name nor any principal altar; the celebration of his
feast-day was restricted. Many causes pass speedily through this stage;
others, through subsidence of interest or devotion, never get beyond it.

The place of miracles

In an essay on holiness it is unnecessary to go into all the detailed
legislation concerning the process of "making" saints. The regulations
alter and are likely to be altered again. Since they are laid down by the
Pope, the Pope can, in selected cases, dispense with them. Miracles
worked by God through the intercession of the saints were not always a
requirement for the canonisation of martyrs and there have been both
confessors and martyrs canonised in this century without investigation
into alleged miracles. St. Thomas More's cause is an instance. Normally
after a canonisation all the materials forming the enquiry and leading
up to it are printed and made available for inspection as freely as the
documents on an established cure at Lourdes.

The place of miracles must not be overstressed. In earlier and simpler
times there was great emphasis put upon them as a confirmation from
heaven of a human judgement liable always to error. No one can explain
why the intercession of certain saints seems more effective and consistent
than that of others. St. Anthony of Padua has long been an unchal-
lenged favourite; *The Times* personal column regularly records the
gratitude of clients of St. Jude; for more than two decades Thérèse of
Lisieux enjoyed astonishing popularity: religious Orders, continental
cities, the hill towns of Umbria and Southern Italy, ancient guilds and
modern societies, all have their chosen saints on whose prayers local

[1] Cf. *The Miracles of King Henry VI: being an account and translation of twenty-three miracles taken
from the MS in the British Museum* (Royal 13c. viii) *with Introductions by Father Ronald Knox and
Shane Leslie* (Cambridge, 1923).

reliance is placed. Abuses occur; at times they are suppressed; Roman control, though strict, cannot always be effective, any more than the machinery of other centralised organisations. But in its source and manifestation devotion to the saints remains the same in our time as in the earliest days of Christianity.

Whatever fate the world or the individual may suffer, the saints remain heroes, protectors, patrons, friends and intercessors; they are the honoured members of the Christian community, examples of virtue that all, by their baptism into Christ, are pledged to pursue; their task is not completed with their death, nor their power for good curtailed by it; they do not stand between the Christian and Christ, but often give him an introduction to His ways, for they walked in His company in the world and live in His presence in heaven; with them we invoke God as our Father, and by the assistance of their prayers seek to carry out His will on earth. As long as the Church remains a human as well as a divine body they will have their place in her converse with God.

Holiness

in

The Lutheran Tradition

by

REGIN PRENTER

Regin Prenter, D.D., was born in 1907 in Denmark. He studied at Copenhagen University, the University of Strasbourg, University of Bonn, Lincoln Theological College and at King's College, Cambridge. He is now Professor of Dogmatics at Aarhus University. Among his best-known works outside Denmark are *Spiritus Creator* (Luther's doctrine of the Holy Spirit), *The Spirit and the Word*, *Le Saint-Esprit et le Renouveau de l'Eglise*, *Creation and Redemption*, *The Church's Faith* and *Der Cormherzige Richter*.

Justification by faith and Biblical authenticity

THE doctrine of justification by faith holds a unique position in the Lutheran tradition. It is generally regarded as the article by which the Church stands or falls.[1]

Non-Lutherans are often bothered by this apparently one-sided emphasis. If justification is everything, what then becomes of sanctification? If the forgiveness of sins constitutes the entire process of salvation, it looks as if there was no renewal of life in Jesus Christ: the sinner justified by faith remains at once sinner and righteous until his death. Thus it seems as though there is no room whatsoever in the Lutheran tradition for a genuine understanding of sanctity. Catholic critics of Lutheranism in the past have often brought this accusation against it. And if the doctrine of justification by faith alone were in fact isolated in such a heretical manner, the accusation would certainly hold true.

It must, however, be strongly emphasised that this is not what the Lutheran tradition understands by the *articulus stantis et cadentis ecclesiae* (the article by which the Church stands or falls). This does not mean, of course, that this article is the only one to be taught. It means, however, that this article is fundamental in as much as it concerns the very foundation of the sinner's relationship to most Holy God. It therefore constitutes a criterion by which to test whether or not a particular doctrine or practice is in harmony with the centre of the Biblical message of salvation. If there is a particular Lutheran conception of sanctity (and this may well be questioned), the specifically Lutheran element would be precisely this testing of its Biblical authenticity by means of the fundamental doctrine of justification. Any conception of the sinner's holiness which contradicts the very foundation of his relation to God, i.e. his justification before God by faith in Jesus Christ alone, certainly has no room in the Lutheran tradition.

---

[1] Justification by faith is the absolving of man from the consequences of his sin by his faith in Christ [Ed.]

Righteousness and holiness

God is holy. This statement is the starting point for any understanding of man's sanctity. God has manifested His holiness among men in Jesus Christ, His Only Son, made man: "For thou only art holy; thou only are the Lord . . . O Christ . . ." *He* is the Holy One among sinners. His holiness shines from the Cross where He takes away the sins of the world. "O, Lord God, Lamb of God, Son of the Father, that takest away the sins of the world, have mercy upon us . . . Thou that takest away the sins of the world, receive our prayer. Thou that sittest at the right hand of God the Father, have mercy upon us. For thou only art holy."[1]

His holiness is God's own holiness, for He is the Son of the Father. But we are sinners, we are rebels against God, we have lost the right to appear before Him, to live in His sight. Holiness is participation in the holiness of Jesus Christ, the Holy One. We have lost that right, we are under the judgement of God.

There is, therefore, no possibility of our sharing in the holiness of Jesus Christ, unless God annuls His condemnation of us as sinners, unless He gives us back the right to appear before Him and this He can do only by accepting the perfect sacrifice of faith and obedience offered by His Only Son on our behalf. This God has done, once and for all, by raising the crucified Lamb of God from the grave and in exalting Him to the heavenly throne, where He is our eternal advocate and intercessor (Rom. 8.31-34). He, the Lamb of God who sits at the right hand of God the Father, is our righteousness, i.e. He grants to us sinners the right to appear before God, the right to pray to God, the right to hope that God will grant our prayers, the right to live in the service of God. God proclaims this justification of the sinner through Jesus Christ in the Gospel, and the sinner receives it through faith in the promise of the Gospel of God.

This righteousness before God, the result of our justification by faith alone, enables us to receive holiness from God, to participate in the holy life and death of Jesus Christ. Therefore righteousness goes before holiness.

Justification takes place in baptism which is the new birth by water and spirit. Sanctification, the growth of that life which is born in Baptism, the growing participation in the divine-human life of Jesus Christ, the crucified and risen Lord, is accomplished in a sacramental

---

[1] *Gloria in excelsis.*

manner comprehending the baptism at the start of Christian life, never to be repeated and the Eucharist, repeated again and again, until its consummation in the Kingdom of Heaven. This indicates the proper relationship between righteousness and holiness. Righteousness is the fruit of the new birth by water and spirit. Holiness is that quality of the spiritual life which was born in Holy Baptism. The holy life must be born in order to grow and ripen. Or, to put it differently, we must have access to that spiritual realm where holiness dwells in order to experience its reality.

Both righteousness and holiness are unmerited gifts flowing from the free grace of God. They are both a participating in the perfect life of Jesus Christ. This is the reason why the sacraments are a necessary means for obtaining righteousness and holiness. Man cannot justify himself in the sight of God, he could not even if he were morally perfect. For the will to justify oneself is the essence of sin, that culmination of self-love which changes moral perfection into immoral pride. And man cannot make himself holy. For the will to achieve holiness by one's own effort represents false holiness, the unholy self-assertion which refuses to receive anything from our gracious Lord. The sinner must be baptised into the name of Jesus Christ in order to be born into a righteous life before God. And the baptised child of God must receive the bread of life and the cup of blessing, i.e. must participate in the perfect sacrifice of Jesus Christ at His table, in order to grow in a holy life.

If we distinguish between *holiness* and *sanctity* we may say that sanctity includes both righteousness and holiness. A "holy" person who thinks he may claim a holiness of his own, i.e. a holiness which deserves God's recognition, is not a saint (*sanctus*), but an ungodly pharisee (Luke 18.10-14). "And base things of the world, and things which are despised, hath God chosen, yea, and things which are not, to bring to nought things that are: That no flesh should glory in His presence. But of Him are ye in Christ Jesus, who of God is made unto us wisdom and righteousness, and sanctification, and redemption: That, according as it is written, He that glorieth, let him glory in the Lord." (1 Cor. 1.28-31) A saint is a person who has ceased to live for himself in order to live in Jesus Christ. The saints are the holy Church of God: "Paul, called to be an apostle of Jesus Christ through the will of God, and Sosthenes our brother. Unto the church of God which is at Corinth, to them that are sanctified in Christ Jesus, called to be saints, with all that in every place call upon the name of Jesus Christ our Lord, both theirs and ours." (1 Cor. 1.1-2)

Passive or receptive sanctity

In his famous *Commentary on the Epistle to the Galatians*, Martin Luther says that Christian sanctity is passive: *Christiana sanctitas est passiva*.[1] And he explains this by saying that you and I, the Church, a city or nation, are holy (*sanctus*), not through an active but through a passive or receptive sanctity, i.e. because we receive holy or spiritual gifts (*sancta*) such as the vocation to the ministry of the Church, the Gospel, Baptism, etc. It is through these gifts that saints are made.

This passivity, however, does not mean inaction but receptiveness. In receiving this passive sanctity man does not remain idle. On the contrary, he is striving all the time. Receiving is in itself a specific sort of labour. The scholastic terms *passive* and *active* used by Luther must not be interpreted in a psychological sense, as if a man in receiving passive sanctity were psychologically inactive. Active means productive with regard to God's recognition, i.e. deserving, and passive means receptive to God's recognition, i.e. sanctity freely received.

Passive sanctity, therefore, indicates the righteousness of faith which brings about holiness in deeds of love (Gal. 5.6) or the holiness of love which springs from the righteousness of faith (Rom. 6.22). The passive or receptive character of Christian sanctity marks its Godward relationship. Before God we are always passive for we are His creatures. "Nay but, O man, who art thou that replieth against God? Shall the thing formed say to him that formed it, Why hast thou made me thus? Hath not the potter power over the clay, of the same lump to make one vessel unto honour, and another unto dishonour?" (Rom. 9.20-21)

This is to say that receptive sanctity cannot enter man, unless self-righteousness and self-love have been destroyed. The righteousness of faith proclaimed in the Gospel, presupposes the condemnation of man's self-righteousness. And the holiness of love communicated to us through our participation in the sacrificial self-surrender of the crucified Jesus Christ shatters our self-love.

Thus passive sanctity includes patiently enduring God's judgement upon our self-righteousness and God's mortification of our self-love. The sign of this suffering which marks the contrast between sanctity and morality, i.e. between the perfection given by God's grace and the perfection achieved by man's effort, is the Cross. Passive sanctity is

---

[1] *W.A.* XL, 1,70,1. *W.A.* means the Weimar Editions of Luther's works (*D. Martin Luthers Werke*. Kritische Gesammtausgabe. Weimar, 1883.)

conformity with the crucified Christ. "For if ye live after the flesh, ye shall die: but if ye through the Spirit do mortify the deeds of the body, ye shall live." (Rom. 8.13)

This element of suffering may be called the ascetic aspect of Christian sanctity. It is well known that the Lutheran tradition took up a very negative attitude towards monastic life. The former monk Martin Luther saw in the *via compendii* at which the inhabitants of the monasteries aimed, a false, meritorious holiness contrary to the grace of God offered in the Gospel. After having left the monastery he vehemently attacked the ideals of monastic life in many of his writings. And in the Churches which were reformed according to the Lutheran pattern the monasteries disappeared almost completely.

This, however, did not mean that the ascetic aspect of Christian sanctity was denied by him. It remained an essential element in the process of justification and sanctification. But it was reinterpreted in the light of the new understanding of the Gospel and of justification by faith alone. Mortification is no longer seen as a praiseworthy human work supported and protected by divine grace, but it is seen in the form of divine punishment, the cross laid upon man by God as His judgement and a means of grace, an act combining God's judgement and forgiveness, and this is man's justification. Thus man is judged by God through His law in order that man may need and seek the forgiveness of God according to the Gospel. In judging man God performs a work alien to His nature (*opus alienum*) in order to prepare His real purpose (*opus proprium*), and both works are accomplished in and through the crucified and risen Jesus Christ. To be judged by God in the very process of justification is, then, to take upon oneself that cross of Christ through which God offers salvation. To carry the cross of Christ as one's own cross means, first of all, to judge oneself, to accept the true and just judgement of God upon the sinner; for on the Cross Christ Himself suffered the judgement of God the Father upon fallen mankind. Self-condemnation is the core of that repentance which is essentially one with faith in the crucified and risen Lord.

But that self-condemnation which is simply the acceptance of God's judgement in obedience and faith does not cease to exist after man's justification. The saint, i.e. the man justified by faith in Christ and made a partaker of His holy life, remains a sinner until his death. Only in the resurrection from the dead will he become a perfect saint, without any "remaining sin", i.e. moral or psychological effects of original sin, to repent of or fight against.

This is the meaning of the formula that the saint is at the same time righteous and sinful – righteous as one accepted by God through His forgiving mercy and sinful as a person who, though living the saintly life of a forgiven sinner and receiving from the Holy Spirit the power to live a new life, still carries this remaining sin, judged and fought against by Holy God. As one who remains until his death at the same time righteous and sinful, the Christian saint must continually carry the cross of God's judgement in his own self-condemnation. The growth of the new life in Christ does not absolve the saint from repenting and fighting against this remaining sin. On the contrary, the more the saint grows in the new life of faith and hope and love, the more he will receive spiritual eyes with which to perceive sin, a new heart to sense it, and a new will to overcome it.

A profound sense of guilt and a relentless struggle against sinful desire are not the signs of a weak and imperfect sanctity; on the contrary they are evidence of a high degree of saintliness. I think that Martin Luther would have appreciated a story which I once heard from an Orthodox theologian about a Russian anchorite who, because of his holy life, was greatly admired by his disciples. On his death-bed he confessed with grief that he had only just begun to understand the immense depth of his sin and guilt . . . and it was only then that his disciples knew with certainty that he was a saint.

Humility and acceptance of the judgement of God are one and the same thing. It is not so much a virtue which man can achieve, as his destiny to which he has to submit. Humility is not a human exercise, but a divine judgement, and as such it forms an essential part of passive sanctity, both in the form of confession of sin (repentance) and as a struggle against sin (mortification). In this struggle to eliminate the last remnants of sin, mortification of the flesh is not a human activity that can be added to divine grace. The forgiveness of sins is a divine gift. The only power which can fight and win the war against evil desires is faith in God's forgiveness for the sake of Jesus Christ. All other attempts to fight against remaining sin are defeated from the outset, because of their synergistic[1] nature; they compromise between sanctity and morality, between divine grace and human self-realisation. Morality indeed is not contrary to sanctity. It is different. Morality does not make a man into a saint. But a saint makes morality serve God's will. One of the principles which Martin Luther asserted again and again is

[1] Doctrine that human will and the Divine Spirit are two efficient agents that cooperate in regeneration. [Ed.]

this: "Good works do not make a man good. But a good man performs good works."

Thus both in justification and in sanctification God works in us through the Cross of Jesus which He puts upon us. And we receive this gift of God through patiently enduring His work in us. This is passive sanctity. In one of his disputations on justification, Luther summarises this truth in the following manner: "Justification includes the following elements: we are reputed righteous by faith for Christ's sake, and no sin, either past or present, in the flesh, is imputed to us, but is remitted completely as though it had never been committed. This faith is accompanied by the birth of the new creature and by the struggle against the sins of the flesh, which are both forgiven and overcome through faith in Christ."[1]

The flesh of which Luther speaks is neither the body nor the bodily lusts. It is the selfish heart of the disobedient and unbelieving sinner, the very centre of that pride and self-love which wants to live without God and which so deserves the destiny created by its own standards, i.e. that evil desire which Luther, adopting the Augustinian and Scholastic terminology and interpreting it in a new manner, calls concupiscence: to seek oneself and one's own interests before anything else. It is Christ alone who has conquered that enemy and who still is able to conquer it. This is why faith in Christ, or rather, that faith in which Christ Himself is present and acting, is the source of both the remission of sins and the overcoming of sin. Thus "justified through grace we perform works", and "Christ Himself works all things in us".[2]

But it is only by the power of the Holy Spirit that the living Christ is present in our faith. Finally, therefore, passive sanctity means suffering. "Now it is certain that neither Christ nor the righteousness of Christ can be grasped through our works, since He is outside us and foreign to us. But faith which is poured into our hearts by our listening to Christ, this can grasp Christ."[3]

Thus passive sanctity, our righteousness and holiness before God, comes from outside us through the external work of the Gospel, which proclaims Jesus Christ as our only righteousness and holiness, and enters our heart through the operation of the Holy Spirit. But that Spirit fights the flesh. "The flesh lusteth against the Spirit, and the Spirit against the flesh: and these are contrary the one to the other . . ." (Gal. 5.17). This war between the Spirit and the flesh makes our sanctity a passive

---

[1] *W.A.* XXXIX, *I*, 83, 35-40.   [2] *W.A.* XXXIX, 46, 18-19.
[3] *W.A.* XXXIX, 83, 24-27.

I

sanctity. We must die in order that Christ may live in us. "That we hate ourselves and condemn concupiscence in choosing charity is not our own accomplishment, but it is the gift of God. Therefore, he says that God condemned and destroyed sin in the flesh. And He works our destruction through His Spirit, through faith in Christ, which is poured into our hearts."[1] This is how Luther explains Rom. 8.3 in his lectures of 1515-1516. It is a very striking description of the nature of sanctity or of the ascetic element in Christian sanctity.

The two dimensions of passive sanctity

As we have seen, passive sanctity comprehends both righteousness and holiness. The righteousness of faith includes the righteousness of repentance or self-condemnation. And the holiness of love includes the holiness of mortification. We may therefore speak of two dimensions of passive sanctity, the interior or spiritual, and the exterior or corporal.

In his early days as a professor, when he was still a monk, Luther, in talking about the cross of the Christian, mainly emphasised the *inner cross*. And in so doing he often quoted late mediaeval mystics, like Tauler, Thomas à Kempis, the *Theologia Germanica* and other writings. However, in emphasising the passive character of the inner cross, Luther dissociates himself clearly from all sorts of mystic techniques. The inner cross is not the result of any kind of spiritual exercise. It is participation in that feeling of guilt and punishment which befell the crucified Lord who bore the sins of the world. The inner cross, therefore, is what Luther in his German tongue calls *Anfechtung* (dereliction), in Latin *tentatio*. It is extremely difficult to find the right equivalent in modern English. The words found in most of the usual dictionaries, like *scruple, inner conflict, temptation* and the like, are all more or less misleading. *Anfechtung* is that dereliction, that experience of eternal damnation which takes possession of man's conscience, when God hides Himself and His grace from man and nothing but God's holy wrath, His uncompromising condemnation of the sinner, remains. "My God, my God, why hast thou forsaken me?" is the true expression of *Anfechtung*, the inner cross, and the most perfect form of passive sanctity. For in taking upon Himself that suffering which is the proper suffering of the Lamb of God, bearing the sins of the world, the Son of God manifested the depth of His Father's sacrificial love. The cry of *Anfechtung* does not spring from that separation from God which is the essence of sin. On the contrary. In his separation from Holy

[1] *W.A.* LVI, 360, 2-6.

God the sinner does not feel the wrath of God. It is the character of sin to feel quite happy without God. If faith and repentance are but two aspects of the same attitude towards God, the same must be true of unbelief and impenitence. The genuine *Anfechtung* of the crucified Lord therefore springs from His eternal love for His heavenly Father. That same eternal divine love which bids Him take upon Himself the guilt of all His human brothers and sisters also makes Him feel the eternal damnation of all sinners with an intensity which no other human being has ever experienced. The *Anfechtung* which a sinner who believes in the crucified Christ may experience from time to time is only a pale shadow of the real *Anfechtung* of the Son of God bearing the sins of the world on the Cross.

If this is so, it becomes clear that all kinds of *Anfechtung* are signs of God's love and not of His anger. If we experience something of that despair which made Jesus cry in the words of the Psalm: "My God, my God, why hast thou forsaken me" (Mark 15.34; Ps. 22.1), it does not mean that God has really abandoned us. It means on the contrary that He allows us for a while to look down into the mysterious depth of His eternal love for His Son. In this context we must examine more closely young Luther's ideas of this dereliction, this *resignatio ad infernum*. If we really love God, i.e. if God allows us to share His Son's eternal love for Him, we also love the will of God, even if He chooses to send us to hell, to leave us in eternal damnation.

But the *resignatio ad infernum* does not mean that the man who does not cease to love God, even if God appears to will his eternal damnation, really goes to hell. For if out of the love for God he no longer fears hell, he will also discover this: where that love prevails hell has ceased to be; it has been changed into heaven. That was what happened when Christ descended into hell and the same thing happens again when the Christian, participating in the love of Christ for the Heavenly Father, spiritually (i.e. in the *Anfechtung*) descends into hell. "If you have dwelt with Him three days in hell you will also dwell with Him in heaven eternally."

In the Finnish Lutheran tradition a beautiful hymn gives wonderful expression to this dialectic of *Anfechtung* and faith:

> I look into the mild eyes of Jesus
> And if He rejects me,
> while sinking
> yet I look
> into the mild eyes of Jesus.

In his *Operationes in Psalmos* (1519-1521) Martin Luther elaborates this theology of *Anfechtung* in a manner unparalleled, I think, in the history of ascetic theology. At one point he explains that during the *Anfechtung* what is felt and experienced (hell, eternal damnation) and what really happens (salvation) are different. "It is felt otherwise than the way it happens, when carnal man is touched by God's work unto salvation, according to 1. Sam. 2.6: 'The Lord killeth, and maketh alive: he bringeth down to the grave, and bringeth up.' Isaiah (28.21) has beautifully depicted the allegorical operation of God 'that He may do his work, His alien work: and bring to pass His act, His alien act'. As if Isaiah were saying: 'Although He is God of life and salvation and those are His proper works, yet He kills and destroys works which are alien to His nature, yet through which He makes His way to His proper work. For He kills our wills in order to establish His own will in us.'"[1] Commenting upon Psalm 22.8-9, Luther says that just as Christ through the contact of His holy body has sanctified the water of Baptism, so He has through His own experience sanctified for us all the waters of *Anfechtung*. "If through the contact of His most clean body He has sanctified all waters for the baptism of regeneration, how much more ought we to believe that He, through the contact of His most pure will and spirit, has sanctified all those heavy waters of the flood, the sufferings and troubles, for our entering into eternal salvation."[2]

Thus passive sanctity teaches man to look upon his own distress with the eyes of God. What he feels and experiences as death, damnation and hell before God, is nothing but life, forgiveness and salvation. "Therefore the words of this verse – Ps. 3.3: 'But Thou, O Lord, art a shield for me: my glory, and the lifter up of mine head' – are not of nature, but of grace, not of free will, but of a most strong spirit of faith, which, looking through the darkness of tempest, death and hell acknowledges the God who abandons as supporter, the God who persecutes as helper, the God who condemns as saviour."[3]

Luther never gave up the theology of the cross. In the *Commentary on Genesis* (1535-1545), compiled by some of his disciples, we find many descriptions of the inner cross similar to those quoted from his early writings. "But when, in our own case, the Red Sea – that is death, sin and hell are in the way, then the power of God and the infirmity of man are joined and united: omnipotence is associated with nothingness and

---

[1] *W.A.* V, 63, 33.   [2] *W.A.* V, 619, 14.
[3] *W.A.* V, 82, 14.

extreme weakness, and yet the powerless are impelled to do impossible and incredible things."[1]

But it is characteristic of Luther's teaching as a reformer that the exterior or corporal dimension of cross-bearing comes to receive more and more emphasis in his understanding of passive sanctity. When he was still an Augustinian monk under the influence of late mediaeval mysticism, he knew from personal experience the cross of the troubled conscience, the *Anfechtung*. Later, when he had left the monastic life behind him in order to proclaim the gospel of the *vocation*, the good news that Gracious God may be served in an ordinary, everyday job in the world, with no less dedication and holiness than in a monastery, he came more and more to learn a different kind of cross-bearing: the sufferings caused by the many evil people in the world who will not allow the faithful servants of God to perform their duty. Thus a good king will suffer from the disloyalty of his subjects. Parents will suffer from the disobedience of their children. The pastor will suffer from the ungodliness of his people. There is no vocation which can be faithfully performed without cross-bearing of this kind. "Therefore, do not bother how you may find sufferings. That will be all right! Be a pious Christian, curate, vicar, citizen, peasant, nobleman, lord, and perform your duty diligently and faithfully. Let the Devil worry how he may find a piece of wood in order to make a cross for you, and the world where it may find twigs to make a birch for your skin."[2] Through these sufferings God breaks down our "old man", our flesh. They are therefore a real cross, they are true mortifications. In commenting upon the story of the sacrifice of Isaac (Gen. 22.3), Luther says: "Having received the commandment, he does not see anything but this alone. In it all things die: Sarah, the family, the home, Isaac. This is the real mortification: to walk in sackcloth and ashes . . . From this commandment springs an immeasurable and deep pain: to lose a son who had been asked for with so many prayers and tears, and with him the hope and the glory, that he had expected to become the father of the blessed seed. Yet he recovered from this suffering and convinced himself that he would get another heir, if not during his lifetime, then after his death. Likewise Sarah, according to Chapter 16, recovered, thinking: I shall not be mother of that heir, I have not been worthy of that. There will be another woman, Hagar my maid. If only God will grant us a son anyway. Those are real mortifications which do not take place in deserts outside human society, but within the family and the State. Through them, therefore,

[1] *W.A.* XLIII, 519, 27.   [2] *W.A.* 11, 412, 23.

the obedience of Abraham may be tested down to the most intimate depth of the heart."[1]

Luther firmly maintained that the *exterior* cross, the sufferings laid upon us in ordinary work, results in true sanctity. And since all Christians have their vocation, and no vocation lacks its specific cross, the passive form of sanctity in this exterior dimension is common to all Christians. It is not a sanctity for spiritual experts, it is not a sanctity to be sought in deserts or monasteries. It is the passive sanctity of ordinary life. This universality of the exterior cross compels Luther to count the holy cross as one of the signs of the Church. In his *About the Councils and the Church*, he lists seven signs of the Church: The Word of God, Baptism, the Eucharist, the keys, the ministry, prayer and – the holy cross.

The two dimensions of passive sanctity, however, cannot be separated. Because man as soul and body is living in both dimensions, his sin and selfishness are active in thoughts, words and deeds, and his old Adam must be put to death both in his exterior and in his interior life. It is typical of Luther's attitude to man that he does not regard his inner life, his soul and spirit, as nearer to true sanctity than his exterior life, the works of his body. Luther, of course, knows that the Spirit is invisible and His work hidden. For the Spirit is God Himself. But the hidden spirituality of God has no greater affinity with that which in Biblical metaphysics is commonly understood as the spiritual, the inward, the incorporeal, the ideal, than it has with the outward and visible, with the body. Because the work of the Spirit is to mediate the reality of the bodily incarnated Son of God, the Spirit of God has special affinity with the outward and the visible. "Spirit, spiritual entity or thing is (and is called) anything which comes from the Holy Spirit, be it as corporeal, external, visible as ever may be. And again: flesh, carnal is anything which comes from the natural power of man without the Spirit be it as inward and invisible as ever may be."[2]

This anti-spiritual but truly Biblical conception of man as body, soul and spirit, forms the background of the two-dimensional character of passive sanctity according to the Lutheran tradition.

Holiness distinguished from sanctity

If we distinguish between sanctity and holiness as I have suggested earlier, then sanctity comprehends both righteousness and holiness. The passive character of sanctity which we have been dealing with in

[1] *W.A.* XLIII, 213, 29.   [2] *W.A.* XXIII, 203, 7.

the preceding section is due to the fact that the righteousness of the Christian is the righteousness of faith in Christ. That is why God must destroy our own righteousness in order to grant us the eternal righteousness of Jesus Christ through faith. In the opening of his *Commentary on the Epistle to the Romans*, Luther says: "The main purpose of this Epistle is to destroy and pull out and disperse any wisdom and righteousness of the flesh (i.e. anything which is considered as such in the judgement of men and even of ourselves), even though it is done with all one's heart and with a sincere intention, and to plant and establish and magnify the sin (even though it is not or is not held to be sin.)"[1] And Luther explains this paradoxical statement in alluding to Jeremiah 1.10: "As He says through Jeremiah: 'to root out, and to pull down, and to destroy', namely everything which is in us (i.e. which pleases us outside ourselves and in ourselves) 'and to build, and to plant', namely everything which is outside ourselves and in Christ. And so with the image in Daniel of the stone destroying the statue. For God wants to save us not through our own, but through an external righteousness and wisdom, which does not come from us nor is born of us, but comes into us from somewhere else, which does not spring from our soil, but comes from Heaven. Therefore, the external and alien righteousness must be taught above all. And thus our own and personal righteousness must be rooted out in advance."[2]

Thus mortification is an essential part of justification by faith in Christ and forms the passive element in Christian sanctity, the bearing of the cross of Christ, the dying with Him in order to rise with Him. "Therefore we are buried with him in baptism into death: that like as Christ was raised up from the dead by the glory of the Father, even so we also should walk in newness of life." (Rom. 6.4)

Passive sanctity, we learn from the apostle, is the beginning of an active holiness, a new life. Or as Luther generally puts it: faith in Christ, by which we are justified before God by receiving a righteousness which is not our own, but the alien righteousness of Jesus Christ, is not a dead faith, but a living faith which works by love (Gal. 5.6).

Luther's most famous description of this active holiness of faith working by love is the passage from his *Preface to the Epistle to the Romans*, which played a decisive role in the conversion of John Wesley. "Faith is

---

[1] *Ficker II*, 1,1. *Ficker II* means *Luthers Vorlesung über den Römerbrief* 15153 *1515/1516*. Herausgegeben von Johannes Ficker, 4. Auflage. II, Die Scholien. Leipzig, 1930.
[2] *Ficker II*, 2, 3.

not that human fancy and dream, which some people regard faith to be and fall into that error that you must do the good works with the purpose of obtaining righteousness and bliss through them, when they discover that no amendment of life or good works follow, though they may hear and speak a lot of faith. What follows is that they, listening to the Gospel, are absent from it, producing by their own power this thought in the heart: I believe! This they consider to be genuine faith. But since it is nothing but a human thought and fiction, which the inmost heart has never experienced, it does not work anything and no amendment follows. No, faith is a divine work in us, which changes us and regenerates us in God (John 1) puts the old Adam to death and makes of us quite different men in heart, courage, mind and in all strength, and brings the Holy Spirit with it. Oh, faith is a living, active, energetic powerful thing! It is impossible for it not to do good actions continually. It does not ask whether good works are to be done; for before you may ask the question faith has already done such works, and is all the time doing good works. A person who does not do such works is a person without faith. He fumbles and looks around him for faith and good works, and yet he does not know what faith nor what good works really are, though he talks and twaddles a lot of words about faith and good works. Faith is a living, tried confidence in the grace of God, so certain of God that it may die for it a thousand times. And such confidence and knowledge of divine grace makes a man joyful, brave and cheerful toward God and all creatures, which is the work of the Holy Spirit through faith. Thus without compulsion he is made willing and joyful in doing good to everybody, serving all people, enduring everything in order to love and to praise God, who has shown him such grace. This is to say that it is impossible to separate works from faith, yea, no more possible than to separate burning and shining from fire."[1]

The activity of faith through the works of love is holy because it is the work of the Holy Spirit. This active holiness is characterised by two features, the first of which is wonderfully brought out in the above passage.

1. Active holiness is spontaneous. Willingly, joyfully, cheerfully without any intention of gaining anything for himself, he who serves God acts in faith. This spontaneity is the fruit of the righteousness of faith. Because man is already righteous before God through faith in Christ, he simply cannot act in order to become righteous. He cannot strive to

[1] *Vorreden zur Heiligen Schrift.* Durchgesen und herausgegeben von Wilhelm Heinsius. München, 1934, pp. 82-83.

obtain that which has already been given him. But he may act spon-
taneously, willingly, joyfully, forgetting himself, out of pure gratitude
towards God. This absence of selfish aims in the spontaneous activity
of faith is precisely what makes it holy, i.e. a God-loving, God-praising
activity.

2. Active holiness is directed by the commandments of God. This
feature is clearly brought out in Luther's writings *About Good Works*
(1520). The first sentence of that book runs: "First of all we must learn
that there are no good works except those which God has ordered, just
as there are no sins except those which God has forbidden."[1] This does
not mean that the works which God has ordered are works of the law,
i.e. works which God's law compels us to do, so that we perform the
works of the law in order to avoid the punishment which the law has
fixed on any transgression, or in order to obtain the reward which the
same law promises to those who fulfil it. If good works were works
imposed upon our will by the power of the law, they would no longer be
those spontaneous, free works of love of which Luther writes in his
Preface to the Epistle to the Romans. Certainly the law, both natural law
and the commandments of the law found in the Scriptures, describes
the works which God wants to be done, the works which He has ordered;
insofar as the works of the law and the ordered works of which Luther
speaks at the beginning of *About Good Works* are the same works. But
the manner in which they are performed is essentially different in the
two cases. The works done under the compulsion of the law, motivated
by the desire for reward or (and) by the fear of punishment, are not
good works in the proper sense of the word. They are necessary works,
and they are right works, because God orders them to be done. But they
are not *good* works, because the heart, dominated by desire for reward
and fear of punishment, i.e. by selfishness, is not a good and obedient
heart, but an evil and disobedient heart. But the works of faith, done
by the believer whose heart is dominated by gratitude and joy because
of God's unmerited grace, are free works, they are done with a heart
which pleases God in receiving His gift: the alien righteousness of Jesus
Christ. The heart is different in the two cases — and God tries the heart —
although the works themselves are the same, the works which God has
ordered.

The works of the law are not holy before God (*coram Deo*), but they
are right before men (*coram hominibus*). The good works of faith on the
other hand are holy before God, because faith in Jesus Christ is the only

[1] *W.A.* VI, 204, 13.

righteousness which God acknowledges in a sinner. This is the reason why Luther, in *About Good Works*, speaking of the good works ordered by God, affirms that the highest and noblest good work, which fulfils all God's commandments, is faith. "The chief and highest and most noble work is faith in Christ, as He Himself says (John 6.) When the Jews asked 'What shall we do, that we might work the works of God', he answered 'This is the work of God, that ye believe on Him whom He hath sent'. . . For in this work all works must move and receive from it the influx of their goodness as a loan."[1]

Thus the spontaneity of active holiness and the fact that it is directed by the commandments of God are but two aspects of the same matter. In every action a choice is made from among the many works which God has ordered. A single person cannot in a single instant do all the works ordered by God in all His commandments. A choice has to be made. And that choice always discloses whether man's heart is obedient or not. If the heart is obedient – and only he who believes in Jesus Christ has the obedient heart, because faith in Jesus Christ is the chief and highest and most noble work – then a man does not choose a work which is considered a merit to himself. For he is already righteous before God through his faith in Christ. Therefore he chooses a work which will praise God and serve his neighbour, even though it may be a most insignificant work in the sight of men, a work which does not contain any merit at all. The disobedient heart, i.e. the heart which does not by faith receive Jesus Christ as the only righteousness before God, but on the contrary wants to be righteous before God by its own works, such a heart is bound to choose those works which seem to be meritorious in the sight of God. Such works are self-selected works. Although they are in many cases works which God has required in His law, they are not the works which God orders him to do here and now. For God does not want man to select among the works of the law those works which may profit himself, but to do what lies at hand, i.e. such works as may express man's gratitude to God and his love for his neighbour. These works alone are the works ordered by God. And they are precisely the works which the spontaneous, joyful, cheerful will, born out of the gratitude of faith, must choose among the innumerable works prescribed by God's law, they are what lies at hand.

Such works are holy works, even though the person who acts thus is still a sinner. They are holy works because God has ordered them. They become works of a holy person, i.e. a justified sinner, when they are

[1] *W.A.* VI, 204, 25.

performed in faith, in the spontaneous, joyful, cheerful obedience of a person who is righteous before God by faith alone.

These two signs of active holiness: spontaneity and the fact that it is directed by the commandments of God, allow us to distinguish between the holiness of persons and works before God (*coram Deo*) and the blamelessness of persons and works before men (*coram hominibus*). The works of the law, even though they are done with an unbelieving, disobedient heart, solely from a desire for reward or from fear of punishment, are, if they conform to the requirements of the law of God and the ordinances of human authorities, correct before men. And they will be rewarded in this life with earthly blessings by God and men. Luther calls this human correctness of exterior work, without reference to the obedience and faith of the heart, *secular righteousness*. But this worldly righteousness cannot be called holiness. It has no value before God. Luther writes: "The righteousness which is contrary to this (viz. criminal sin) is that outward manifestation of righteousness which is symbolised by the apes and peacocks and sycamores of Solomon. From this it is clear that a man who is righteous in this sense is a good man in the eyes of men, free from blame and one who escapes from the punishments of the law and gains temporal promises of the law (Rom. 10). Moses wrote, that if man accomplishes the righteousness of the law he shall live by it. Compare Isaiah 1: 'If ye be willing and obedient, ye shall eat the good of the land . . .' Such men are found today, who repent because of pestilence, famine, war and other scourges of God, who then pray, (make professions of faith) to the saints. Thus the worshippers of saints serve because of corporal benefits and priests because of an offering (and monks and nuns likewise) and all those who do many similar things. In short, this is the righteousness which receives its reward here and in the coming life those who practise it will be punished less severely than criminals. Secondly: it does not serve God but itself, it is not the righteousness of the sons, but of the slaves, it is not the righteousness of Christians, properly speaking, but of Jews and Gentiles. And Christians ought not to be encouraged to work it, since it proceeds from fear of punishment and love for one's own comfort, not from love of God."[1]

There is no holiness in secular righteousness, because it is only valid before men and not before God.

But the active holiness which consists in spontaneous works of faith according to God's commandments is holy in the sight of God because

[1] *W.A.* II, 43, 13-18, 24-30.

of that righteousness of faith, of which it is the unmerited fruit. Therefore, man must not doubt but that his works please God if they are done in faith, even though he is still a sinner who lives only by God's forgiving love.

In the disputation *De veste nuptiali* (1537), Luther maintains, apparently, the "un-Lutheran" view that good works assure us of our faith and testify before God and men to its authenticity:

"We admit that it is true that good works assure us and testify before God, men and even ourselves, that we do truly believe, that we are the sons of God and heirs of eternal life in hope."[1] The surprising thing is that Luther says that our works are not only a testimony to others, but also that they are a testimony to our own hearts. "Therefore the works do not only assure others, but even outselves as to our faith, and the holy martyre would certainly not have undergone so many heavy and hard torments, most cruel and refined tortures and deaths, if they had not with certainty known and in their hearts been fully convinced that they were received in grace and that they truly believed."[2] And, later in the same disputation, commenting upon Isaiah 38.1-8, Luther raises the question as to whether a Christian has the right to glory in his own holy life and answers it in the affirmative! "This argument raises the question whether it is allowed to a Christian man to glory, because he has done good works, has lived a decent and holy life and not offended against God's commandments, so that he may say: 'Lord Jesus Christ! Thou knowest that I live rightly according to Thy statutes that I walk in the ways with a simple and right heart.' Thus a Christian has the right, especially if he is a Doctor of the Church, to glory when he lives according to the prescribed word. Yea, we have not only the right, but we have the duty to glory in our life and in the true doctrine against our adversaries, for we ought to be certain that we are in that way of life and that we teach those things which are pleasant to God because of Christ. When we are therefore in this manner 'in the mercy' or under the wings of merciful God, we may justly glory and with certainty establish, that we who follow the true Leader, live a true, holy, pious and righteous life, but the others who do not live according to the prescribed word of God, live an impious and irreligious life to the shame of God's name. This is what is intended in the Psalm: 'Blessed are the undefiled in the way.' (Ps. 119.1). And we are all perfect, undefiled, holy, pure, because we are 'in the mercy' under the shadow of the wings of Christ. And because we are the first fruits of His new creation

---

[1] *W.A.* XXXIX, 1, 292, 25.
[2] *W.A.* XXXIX, 293, 8.

and have the hope of eternal life, I know with certainty that I have acted rightly, that this doctrine is true. Thus it is necessary to confess and glory in the Lord, but I am not justified for that, as St. Paul says: 'I know nothing by myself; yet I am not hereby justified.' For if God decided to remove, to subtract His mercy, and to enter into argument with us, then it would be the end of us, because no flesh is justified before Him and no man is found pure if God's mercy is removed. Therefore Hezekiah did the right thing when he lived according to God's word and under the shadow of His mercy with a pure heart; so we ought to do so also . . ."[1]

The passage just quoted shows us how passive sanctity and active holiness work together, even though there is a certain tension between them. There is such a thing as an active holiness, a really holy life lived by a Christian. But the holiness of this active life is no holiness at all if it is separated from the passive sanctity of faith in Jesus Christ. We cannot glory except in Christ. Our true glory is that righteousness of Christ which we receive as our own through faith. But if we do receive this righteousness we have not only the right, but it is also our duty to glory in its fruits, in our own righteousness and in our own personal life. The astonishing boldness with which Luther, in the passage quoted above, maintains this right and duty of glorying in a holy life must, however, be seen in the light of that dereliction or *Anfechtung*, which is an essential element of passive sanctity. This glorying is a weapon in the fight against that despair which is the real temptation inherent in any *Anfechtung*, and it is God Himself who gives us this weapon. His purpose in sending this dereliction is that we shall emerge from the struggle strengthened, that our faith should be tried like gold in the fire of the *Anfechtung*. If the exhortation to glory in one's holy life were not understood in this context, it would be both superficial and hypocritical. Further, it must be noted that glorying rests upon justification by faith alone. Only the sinner who trusts in Christ's righteousness, which alone gives him the right to appear before God, may without presumption or blasphemy glory in his own holy life. But he has not only the right, but also the duty to glory.

The two dimensions of active holiness

If an active holiness is "faith which worketh by love" (Gal. 5.6), it is obvious that we shall find again here the two dimensions which we

---

[1] *W.A.* XXXIX, I, 303, 5-305, 1.

considered in our treatment of passive sanctity: the interior (Godward) and the exterior (manward). Love, the fruit of faith, is both love for God, our Creator, and love for man, our fellow creature.

In his polemics against monasticism, Luther strongly emphasised the exterior dimension of active holiness. True love for our neighbour leads us into the vocation of ordinary life. The farmer cultivating the soil, the baker making bread, the mother nursing her child, etc., all these lead a much more holy life than monks and nuns who occupy themselves solely with their own perfection. But this does not mean that Luther neglects the interior dimension of active holiness. On the contrary, he speaks of the necessity for prayer with a passion that is shown by few others in the history of Christian spirituality. In his explanation of the third commandment in *About Good Works*, we find one of his characteristic Lutheran treatises on prayer. He says in the *Introduction* to the section about the third commandment that the first commandment speaks about the thoughts of our hearts in relation to God, the second commandment about our words in the same connection, whereas the third commandment shows us how we must behave towards God in our works: "In this third we are shown how we have to conduct ourselves before God in works."[1] The works are three: to hear the mass, to hear the sermon and to pray. The proper hearing of the mass (in 1520 Luther still uses this traditional expression) is to receive the sacrament with a firm faith in the promise of Christ that He is giving us His own body and blood under the forms of bread and wine. "When this faith is really alive then the heart must become joyous and be warmed and melt in the love of God. Then follows praise and thanksgiving from a sweet heart. Therefore the mass is called *Eucharistia* in Greek, i.e. thanksgiving, that praises and thanks God for that comfortable, bountiful, blessed testament, like a man who thanks and praises and is happy because a good friend has given him 1,000 florins or more."[2] The sermon is the proclamation of that very testament according to which we receive the treasure of Christ's body and blood, given and shed for us to our salvation, in the holy Eucharist.

But prayer is a labour that takes up the whole of a man's life and yet he can never pray enough. "Look here once more: if no other good work were ordered, would not prayer only be enough to exercise a man's faith throughout his life? For that work special spiritual directions were given, and formerly some fathers used to pray day and night. Indeed, there is no Christian who cannot find time to pray without ceasing; I

[1] *W.A.* VI, 229, 22.   [2] *W.A.* VI, 231, 4.

am talking of mental prayer, i.e. nobody is so taken up by his work that he cannot, if he wanted, talk to God in his heart while he is working, present to Him his own or other people's distress, ask for help, pray and, in all that exercise, strengthen his faith . . . Where are they now, those who want to know about good works and do them? Let them take before them prayer only and exercise it rightly in faith, then they will find that it is true what the holy fathers have said, that there is no other work as hard as prayer. Murmuring with the mouth is easy, or looks easy. But to fill the words with the sincerity of the heart in diligent devotion, i.e. desire and faith, so that we seriously desire what the words contain and do not doubt that the prayer is heard, that is a great work in the sight of God."[1]

The most important prayer is the corporate prayer of the assembled people of God. "But the prayer which properly speaking falls under this commandment and is called a work of the sabbath day is much better and greater. It must be offered up for the unity of all Christendom, for the distress of all men, enemies and friends, especially for those who are in every parish or diocese."[2] If Christian people would really perform this work properly what could not happen in the Church! "O, if God would allow that some congregation would still hear the mass and pray in that manner, so that an earnest cry of the heart went up to God from the whole people, what immeasurable virtue and help would not follow from such a prayer! What more terrible thing could happen to all evil spirits? What greater work might happen on earth, a work which keeps so many people pious and converts many sinners?"[3]

It is true that the Lutheran tradition has more strongly than most other traditions in Western Christendom emphasised the worldly holiness of the daily vocation, the exterior dimension of active holiness. But it would be quite wrong to overlook the fact that this emphasis is counterbalanced by the immense stress which Luther lays on the work of prayer. It must be clearly stated that modern secular theology with its one-sided emphasis on worldly holiness and its view of prayer as a sign of introversion, has no roots in the genuine Lutheran tradition.

A conclusion

Is there a Lutheran tradition concerning sanctity? In my introductory remarks I questioned the legitimacy of talking about a particular

---

[1] W.A. VI, 234, 31-235, 2; 235, 13-20.   [2] W.A. VI, 237, 34.
[3] W.A. VI, 238, 35.

Lutheran conception of sanctity. After having tried to describe the essential aspects of sanctity, as it has been commonly understood in the Lutheran tradition, and above all by Martin Luther himself, I would be still more hesitant to affirm that there is such a thing as a Lutheran tradition about sanctity. There is certainly a particular vocabulary, due to the situation in which Luther was thinking and writing, and there is also a typical Lutheran emphasis, e.g. the very strong stress laid upon justification by faith alone and the importance of the exterior dimension of both passive sanctity and active holiness. But behind these external particularities, which mainly concern the presentation of thought, we find the great Catholic tradition concerning sanctity. Sanctity is the quality of man's life under God's unmerited grace. Sanctification, the process of becoming saintly or of acquiring sanctity, is a receptive, not a productive function on the part of man: only on the part of God is it productive or creative. But man as he stands in the process of sanctification is both passive and active; he is crucified with Christ and he rises with Him to live a new life.[1] Moreover, this passivity and activity characterise both the exterior dimension of his corporal life and the interior dimension of his spiritual life.

This means that Luther and his followers are rooted in a wider Catholic tradition when they think and speak about sanctity. It is in this wider context of Catholic tradition that we must read them, if we are to understand what they are really saying and to appreciate their particular emphasis.

---

[1] A modern Lutheran saint exemplifying this teaching is the martyr, Dietrich Bonhoeffer. See *World Come of Age* Ed. R. G. Smith, Collins, London, 1967. [Author.]

Holiness
in
The Orthodox Tradition

by

PAUL EVDOKIMOV
(translated from the French by Constance Babington Smith)

K

Paul Evdokimov, Ph.D., Th.D. was born in St. Petersburg in 1901. Professor Evdokimov settled in France in 1923; he is Professor at the Orthodox Theological Institute of St. Sergius in Paris and also teaches at the Ecumenical Institute of the Paris Catholic Institute; he was awarded a D.Honoris Causa at the University of Salonica and he is a member of the International Academy of Religious Science at Brussels. He contributed an article on the Orthodox Church to the French Encyclopaedia, and his books include: *Dostoïevsky et le Problème du Mal, La Femme et le Salut du Monde, L'Orthodoxie, Gogol et Dostoïevsky ou la Descente aux Enfers, Le Sacrement de l'Amour, Les Ages de la Vie Spirituelle* (English translation: *The Struggle with God*), *La Prière de l'Eglise d'Orient, La Connaissance de Dieu selon la Tradition Orientale, La Théologie de la Beauté.*

The concept of holiness

HOLINESS is above all the reverse of everything worldly; it represents the eruption of something utterly different from this world. The words *sacred* and *holy* have, however, in the course of their evolution, broken away from their root and taken on a moral connotation that does not in the least convey their original meaning, which was concerned with ontological significance, or pure being. For example, in the idiom of the present day, expressions such as "a holy purpose", "a sacred duty", "a sacred law", "a holy man", are used with a moral connotation.

The Bible gives us the fundamental truth: God alone is holy; creatures can be so only by derivation. Nothing is holy or sacred by virtue of its own nature, but always by participation in the divine. The Hebrew term *qadosh*, the Greek *agios*, the Latin *sacer, sanctus*, all imply a state of belonging absolutely to God, of being set apart.

The divine act of sanctification or consecration withdraws a being or a thing from the context of its own experience and brings it into communion with the divine energies of grace; this changes its nature and at once brings about an experience, within the natural setting, of the *mysterium tremendum*, a holy trembling before the coming of the divine and its awe-inspiring purity. This is not at all the same thing as fear of the unknown but a mystical sense of awe which accompanies all manifestations of the Transcendent: "I will send my fear before thee, and will destroy all the people to whom thou shalt come," (Ex. 23.27) and again, "Put off thy shoes from off thy feet, for the place whereon thou standest is holy ground." (Ex. 3.5)

In the midst of the world's false standards and ideas, the revelation of a reality that is "innocent" because it is sanctified — which means purified and restored to its original state, to its initial destiny of being a pure receptacle of the divine presence — is an overwhelming one; the holiness of God rests within it and shines through it. Indeed when a place is holy it is holy because of the presence of God. It was thus that the part of the Temple enclosing the Ark of the Covenant was holy, thus are the Scriptures holy (because they bear witness to the presence of Christ in his Word); thus every church is holy since it is there that God dwells, speaks, and gives himself as food. The "kiss of peace" is holy because it puts a seal upon a communion that is shared in Christ. The prophets, the apostles, the "saints" at Jerusalem were holy by virtue of the special graces of their ministries; in the Orthodox Churches a bishop is given the title of "holy brother" and a patriarch is called "his holiness" not by reason of any human qualities he may have, but because of his participation in the unique priesthood of Christ. All those who are baptised and confirmed are "anointed", sealed with the gifts of the Holy Spirit, so that they may be "partakers of the divine nature" (2 Pet. 1.4) and "of his holiness" (Heb. 12.10); it is also in this sense of participation in divine holiness that St. Paul uses the word "saints" for the members of a Christian community.

The Orthodox Liturgy includes some relevant teaching which is very explicit. Before the priest administers the sacrament he pronounces the following words, "The holy things unto them that are holy", and the assembled faithful, as though overwhelmed by this tremendous demand, confess their unworthiness: "One is holy, one, Jesus Christ, is Lord." Christ alone, Christ uniquely, is a Saint by nature. His members are not saints except by means of their participation in his unique holiness.

Another very illuminating example is given by Isaiah: "Woe is me! ... I am a man of unclean lips ... Then flew one of the seraphims unto me, having a live coal in his hand, which he had taken with the tongs from off the altar: And he laid it upon my mouth, and said, Lo, this hath touched thy lips; and thine iniquity is taken away." (Is. 6.5-7) The power of the divine holiness is a devouring flame that consumes all impurity; when it touches a man it purifies him and makes him holy; it brings him into harmony with the holiness of God – even into its likeness. In the Liturgy, at the time of the Communion, the priest brings Isaiah's vision into remembrance, for as he kisses the rim of the chalice, which represents the pierced side of Christ, he repeats the words, "Lo, this hath touched my lips; and mine iniquity shall be taken away, and my sin purged." The spoon which he uses to administer the sacrament is called *lavis* in Greek (meaning "tongs") just as in Isaiah's vision; and the Fathers, in speaking of the Eucharist, say "You are partaking of fire."

From the one divine source ("Be ye holy; for I am holy") there flows forth a stream of every kind of sanctification and participation in the holy. This introduces into the very being of the world an influence that "deprofanes" and "devulgarises". This action of "penetrating" the world is the prerogative of the sacraments, and of those who take part in them, for they show that everything in a Christian life is potentially sacramental or holy, since everything has a destiny in relation to Christ, everything is meant to share in the mystery of the divine presence. Thus at Easter and at the feast of the Transfiguration the fruits of the earth are brought to the Church to be blessed, thereby extending to everything used for food the eucharistic principle of the offering, the gift, and the consecration.

The destiny of water is to participate in the mystery of the Epiphany,[1] that of wood is to be the tree of life and the substance of the Cross. The earth's destiny is to receive into itself the body of the Lord in the repose of Easter Eve, while rock provides the sepulchre for him and the stone that the angel rolled back before the coming of the women with the spices. Water and oil attain to their fulfilment in the sacraments of baptism and unction; wheat and the vine reach theirs in the eucharistic chalice. It is clear that everything centres on the Lord, as though this universal synthesis of all creation were a splendid liturgy. Within this liturgy all the simplest actions of everyday life — drinking, eating, washing, speaking, acting, living — fall into their true place, which is to participate in the holiness of God. "At last all things are the furnishings of our temple instead of our prison" — so, with great truth, said Paul Claudel.

Thus holiness by participation is the restoring, the healing, of nature in relation to Christ, "the return from that which is contrary to nature towards that which truly belongs to it".[2]

Holiness: the healing of nature

"What *is* a heart full of charity?" asks St. Isaac the Syrian. "It is a heart which burns with love for all creation, for men and for demons, for all creatures . . . The man who possesses such a heart is moved by an immense compassion . . . He cannot endure that any sorrow, however trivial, should be inflicted upon any creature. He prays even for reptiles, impelled by the infinite pity aroused in the hearts of those who have been assimilated into God." According to St. Paul all nature is groaning in travail as she awaits the salvation of man, the coming of the holiness which will also be her own redemption — insofar as she is part

---

[1] In the Orthodox tradition the main theme of the Epiphany is the Baptism of Christ. [Ed.]
[2] St. John Damascene, *De Fide Orth.* 1, 30.

of the divine creation (Rom. 8.22). It is the saint who by means of his love reunites the disrupted universe, opening it up to the healing action of grace.

In the light of the Bible, salvation has nothing to do with judgement; it is not the verdict of a jury. The Hebrew verb *yasha* means to set free, to unburden; this, in a more general sense, signifies to deliver or save (from a danger, an illness, death) which more precisely still means to re-establish a living equilibrium, to heal. The noun *yesha*, "salvation", means an entire deliverance accompanied by peace – the consummation of "*shalom*". In the New Testament the equivalent Greek word *sōtēria* comes from the verb *sōzein*, while the adjective *sōs* corresponds to the Latin *sanus*, and it means to bring health to one who has lost it, to save him from death, the natural end of all diseases.

That is why, in the Gospel, the expression "thy faith hath saved thee" means the same thing as "thy faith hath healed thee", the two terms being synonymous for the same act of divine pardon – an act which cures both soul and body in their interdependent unity. In tune with this idea the sacrament of confession in the East is regarded as a "medical treatment", and St. Ignatius of Antioch calls the Eucharist "the healing remedy of immortality" – the antidote to death.

Thus Jesus the Saviour appears as the divine healer, the "bringer of health", saying "They that be whole need not a physician, but they that are sick." Sinners are the sick who are threatened by total death, and the therapeutic meaning of salvation *is* healing, the universal elimination of the germ of corruption, which is mortality. Redemption is seen to be a corollary of the resurrection of the body. "By death he has conquered death"; this physical aspect of salvation means a victory both spiritual and physical as regards all the consequences of the Fall. It is the essence of St. Paul's doctrine of the "new creature".

The new creature

Though man, admittedly, is not at the centre of the astronomers' universe he truly represents its summit, for in man the evolution of the universe has attained to self-awareness. In time, too, man is the climax. Time was at first orientated towards the coming of the Messiah; now, although the King himself has come, his kingdom is still in the future. Ever since Pentecost, time has been leading – so the Church believes – toward the full accomplishment of the Kingdom, and it bears man onward towards his fulfilment as a new creature. This was made possible when God himself became the new Man, the absolute Man, for all to follow.

It is not a case of "repairing" or "reorganising" the old man. The old man is discarded and dies, says St. Paul, while the new man is renewed from day to day. This metamorphosis (*metanoia*), which is the complete change of direction spoken of in the synoptic gospels and called by St. John "the second birth", is a radical event. It is not a new creation but, according to the Fathers of the Church, a return towards the norm, towards nature's true original state. "Oh man, give thought to that which thou art!" exclaims St. Gregory of Nyssa, "Remember thy royal dignity." And St. Paul asks "What is man? . . . Thou madest him a little lower than the angels; thou crownedst him with glory and honour . . . Thou hast put all things in subjection under his feet." (Heb. 2.6-8)

Man, according to the Fathers, is at the same time king, prophet and priest, just as Christ himself was. "King by reason of his mastery over the passions, priest because of his self-immolation, prophet as an initiate into the divine mysteries." Christianity — as testified by the resounding witness of its confessors, martyrs and saints — is messianic, revolutionary, explosive. The Gospel demands the kind of violence that seizes the Kingdom, ravishes the heavens and transforms the old image of the world into the new creation. The new creature, the new man — both of these terms are in fact synonyms for sanctity; as St. Paul says "All . . . [are] called to be saints." Salt of the earth and light of the world, the saints, sometimes conspicuous, sometimes obscure and hidden, go forward as guides and beacons for all humanity.

At the start of the Christian era the martyrs, "friends of the bridegroom who have been sacrificed", were "the blades of wheat which the winds have harvested, and the Lord has garnered them in his kingdom". Then the saints took over the torch from the hands of the martyrs and brought its light to the world. But the call of the Gospel is addressed to all men. If (according to Origen) the Church since the Incarnation is "full of the Trinity", since Pentecost it is full of saints. During the office for the feast of All Saints this overwhelming truth is openly declared: "I sing in honour of all the friends of my Lord, and let any man who desires him join himself to their company." This invitation is extended to each and all: "The cloud of witnesses comes forth to meet us," says St. John Chrysostom, "so as to proclaim itself *urbi et orbi*."[1] The Church's Communion of Saints reflects the holiness

---

[1] To the city and to the world. [Ed.]

of God: "Thy light, O Christ," sings the Church, "shines in the face of thy saints."

In the mystery of his Incarnation God transcends his own transcendence, transcends his effulgent Holiness (according to some of the Fathers, the word "God" comes from the verb "to burn"), and makes his deified humanity consubstantial, immanent, accessible to all men. This is the ultimate act of God's love which Nicholas Cabasilas calls *manikon eros*, God's "mad love" for man: "Henceforth I call you not servants . . . but . . . friends." (John 15.15)

In Old Testament times the few chosen places where God manifested his dazzling presence to men were indicated by theophanies;[1] the "burning bush" was one such holy place. But ever since Pentecost the saints have been entrusted with the entire world so that it may be transformed into a "burning bush" as great as the universe itself. God has said, "The world is mine, and the fulness thereof", and this now means that the world is the dwelling place of his saints in whom he is present.

In the old days man was told, "Put off thy shoes from off thy feet, for the place whereon thou standest is holy ground" (Ex. 3.5); a particular spot in the world was sanctified because the Holiness of God had touched it. But since then there has been a transition to a new order. This may be seen in an ancient icon of St. John the Baptist which shows the saint treading upon an earth soiled by sin, all tangled and overgrown, but everywhere he has stepped the world becomes Paradise once more: "Earth, become pure again, for the feet which have trodden thee are holy."

A man who is said to have a strong personality evinces a particular blend of natural characteristics, certain of them specially pronounced, but in spite of these he usually gives an impression of something already familiar. A saint on the other hand is striking by reason of the uniqueness of his face, and the radiance of his personality, which has a quality of the absolute. He has never been seen before. He cuts right away from the conventional and his newness shocks people and is called "a scandal" and "madness". In the eyes of the Marxist a saint is a useless creature; what is the point of a saint, a "fool in Christ"? But it is precisely this condition of being completely at the disposal of the Transcendent which startles the complacency of a forgetful world.

A saint, even the most hidden of saints "clothed in space and in nakedness", carries upon his frail shoulders the weight of all the world

---

[1] Manifestations or appearances of God to man. [Ed.]

and the darkness of its sin, and protects it from divine justice. While he is mocked by men the saint, by virtue of his tears, draws the divine mercy towards mankind. Furthermore, the saints, in their humility, believe themselves to be "the foremost of sinners" (in the words of the prayer before Holy Communion) and by their love for sinners, by means of their "communion in sin", they can draw these sinners towards a "communion in holiness". Before dying, some hermit or "fool in Christ" prayed the following words as a final Amen to his whole ministry: "That all may be saved, that all the world may be saved."

The thing which always scandalises unbelievers is not that saints exist, but the truly terrible fact that not all Christians are saints. In the characteristic words of Léon Bloy: "There is only one sorrow, that of not being a saint."

The holiness of the Church

"I believe in one holy, catholic and apostolic Church." Thus in A.D. 381 the Council of Constantinople defined the essential characteristics of the Church, and sanctity was thereby declared to be one of them: "Be ye holy; for I am holy." The response to this stupendous demand is the sacramental superabundance of the Church, which never ceases to pray for life-giving grace, so that it may bring water to humanity's arid and desert soil. "Send us of thy most Holy Spirit to sanctify and illumine our souls." "By means of the Holy Spirit all creation is restored to its original state."[1] Christ gave himself for the Church "that he might sancify and cleanse it" (Eph. 5.25-27) and might show forth in it "the One who is", in other words the fact of holiness. The Church does not lack sinners, but she is herself without sin. The dynamic tension within her, between the "already now" and the "not yet", is caused by the mystery of the presence of the Kingdom which precedes but also anticipates its final consummation.

In the Book of Revelation the ultimate fulfilment is foreshadowed: men and angels fall down before the Lamb and sing the thrice-holy hymn, "Holy, Holy, Holy"; here is sanctity in terms of song, the Church transformed into the divine Liturgy itself, and into the everlasting Communion of Saints.

"The splendour of the Trinity shines ever more brightly," so wrote St. Gregory of Nazianzus.[2] In its light, each of the divine persons is seen to play a unique part in the same work of salvation. Thus although

[1] Office prayers for the Feast of the Ascension and for Sunday morning.
[2] *Or.* 31, 26-7.

Christ redeems and integrates all mankind within the unity of his Body, the personal relationship with him should never in any sense be lost within the corporate and impersonal. This is why the Holy Spirit acts in relation to individuals, causing each one to grow up into the fulness of gifts and graces by following a special way intended for him alone. The story of Pentecost makes it clear that grace descended upon each individual member of the group of disciples: "Cloven tongues like as of fire . . . sat upon each of them." (Acts 2.3) At the heart of unity in Christ, the Spirit is diversified: "We are as though merged into one body yet as persons we are divided," says St. Cyril of Alexandria.[1]

As a result of the Fall the action of the Spirit became exterior to nature, thus at the time of the holy baptism in the River Jordan the Spirit descended upon the humanity of Christ; but on the day of Pentecost he became active in human nature from within, thereby establishing the "interior fact" of human sanctity.

The Church is sanctified with the holiness of Christ (Eph. 5.25-27) and by virtue of being the source of the sacraments and of sanctification she brings the Communion of Saints into being. Always, throughout all her history, the Church has defined a clear concept: she is not a society of perfect saints, of the elect and pure alone. Her mystery is to be at the same time "the Church of the penitents, of those who perish", as St. Ephrem says, and also the means of communion between sinners and the "holy things" [the sacraments], of their deifying participation in that which alone is holy. She glorifies the holiness of God, she venerates the "all-holy" Virgin Mary, as well as all the saints – known and unknown – who form her "golden girdle", and she affirms that every "sinner" whose life derives from the life of the Church receives the full measure of sanctity ordained for him.

In speaking of "the Holy Church" one means above all the holiness the Church confers upon her children. The sanctity they receive during their lifetime is hidden in a mystery and a silence seen by God alone, though he may reveal it to others within the Church, and if so then they become widely known through canonisation. Thenceforth they continue their ministry amongst men and in the service of the world.

The origin and development of the veneration of the saints

In the Bible it is the Book of Job that first insists on the intercession of the righteous. "My servant Job shall pray for you: for him will I

---

[1] *In Joan.*, XI; *Patrologia Graeca*, 59, 361.

accept: lest I deal with you after your folly." (Job 42.8) The Book of Job also mentions turning to saints and angels for light and for help. (5.1; 33.23) In the Gospel, Moses and Elijah stood one on either side of Jesus at the Transfiguration, and in speaking of his friends the Lord said, "If any man serve me ... him will my father honour."

Origen[1] echoes St. Paul's teaching on the unity of the saints with Christ; if one member of the Body is honoured all the fellow members rejoice with him. (1 Cor. 12.26) The Church extends over the whole of the earth and also over the heavens. Those who fall asleep in Christ are "present with the Lord." (2 Cor. 5.6-8) Origen maintains that the whole of the Epistle to the Hebrews is inspired by the spirit of the Communion of Saints. (Heb. 1.14; 2.10-11; 13.7) While awaiting the day when God "will be glorified in his saints" these very saints continue their ministry of intercession for the living. The Book of Revelation speaks of the martyrs as being in prayer before the throne of God, as well as being very close to the Lamb. "Blessed are the dead which die in the Lord from henceforth" (Rev. 14.13) [and] "they which are called unto the marriage supper of the Lamb." (Rev. 19.9)

Thus the tradition first took shape from the scriptural idea of the Communion of Saints. The oldest of the early "Christian letters", the *Martyrium Polycarpi*, written in about A.D. 156, mentions a devotional cult aimed at upholding the examples of the saints. The veneration of the martyrs goes back to the anniversaries of the funeral ceremonies which celebrated a martyr's birthday, the date of his birth into eternal life. For a short time martyrs who had escaped death were revered as priests, even though they had not been ordained; this was by reason of the ministry of prayer inherent in their vocation. Those who had died for God remained, in Christ, in communion with the living.

Under Cyprian, in Africa, the Church recognised the posthumous power of martyrs as intercessors before the face of God.[2] This same ministry, during times of persecution, is alluded to in inscriptions on tombs and in the "graffiti" of the catacombs. The martyrs are the "advocates" of the faithful.[3] St. Jerome writes to the mother of Blesilla: "She prays to the Lord for you, and as for me she obtains pardon for my sins."[4]

According to Origen, a martyr is a source of grace for all the faithful,[5] while in times of peace the lack of martyrs enfeebles the Church. The prayer of those on earth and of those in heaven is one and identical; the

---

[1] *De Oratione* II, 2. [2] *De Lapsis*, c. 17. [3] St. Augustine, *P.L.* 38, 1209.
[4] *Epist.* 25. [5] *P.G.* 11, 636; 12, 638.

souls of the martyrs share with the angels in the worship of the faithful.[1] Those who are in heaven continue to take part in the battle waged by the faithful who are still living, since the functioning of salvation is concentrated within one Body only, in which the life blood that circulates is one and the same.

The ideal of martyrdom, of that glorious company consisting of the "friends of the bridegroom who have been sacrificed", and in which "Christ himself fights in person", makes the spirituality of the first centuries unique. The martyr, himself a living representation of the crucified Lord, preaches Christ by giving himself up as a "public spectacle" under the eyes of men and of angels. "Your bodies are pierced through by the sword but your spirit can never be withdrawn from divine love. Suffering with Christ you are consumed by the glowing fires of the Holy Spirit," thus sings the Church. According to an ancient tradition every martyr, at the moment of his death, hears the words that were spoken to the good thief, "Today shalt thou be with me in paradise"; then (so St. John Chrysostom taught) he enters immediately into the Kingdom, so as to exercise his powers of intercession there.

Later, the fact that the Church was protected by law (from the fourth century onwards) did nothing to soften the violence of her message. At once the Holy Spirit substituted for the martyr's "baptism of blood" the "baptism of austerity" of the ascetics and saints. The famous *Life of Saint Anthony* by Athanasius the Great described him as the first to attain to sanctity without tasting martyrdom. From monastic sanctity there emerged the type of the "very likeness" – the living icon of God. Thus the Desert Fathers,[2] confronted as they were by the compromises of the world, were the first to attain to *metanoia*, the "being born again" of the Gospel – a reorientation of the entire functioning of the human being.

The formidable Thebaid, desert cradle of so many spiritual giants, that arid, burnt-up stretch of wilderness, still seems to glow with their light. In the silence of the cells and the caves – the training ground of these "disciples of God" – the birth of the "new creature" came slowly to pass; the restoring, the healing of nature, the glorious advent of the saints. God remains hidden, but he offers his martyrs and his saints as witnesses to be seen by all. The pure in heart see God, and through them God reveals himself.

---

[1] *P.G.* 11, 448; 553.
[2] Monks and hermits living in the deserts mainly in Egypt and Palestine during the third, fourth, and fifth centuries. [Ed.]

The tradition of the ministry of the saints developed gradually. In the third century there had been a firm belief in their intercessions for the Church although, as Origen points out, the Lamb alone blots out sin and the saints do no more than offer up their prayers.[1] Tertullian also stresses that the saints are in no sense "Gods", but simply intercessors.[2] The teaching of the Fathers is very clear and definite: the cult of the saints is a cult of "love and veneration" and the veneration flows onward towards God himself, who is honoured in his servants. Prayers made by the saints are ultimately addressed to God alone, just as the icon of a saint glorifies the divine light reflected in his face. It is true that God does not need the prayers of the saints, yet the Gospel parable of the importunate widow emphasises the need for the dynamic fervour of faith, and then again the prayers of the saints express the communion of mutual love. They are a manifestation of the unity of the Body; they provide a channel for the bestowal of grace; as St. James says, "the effectual fervent prayer of a righteous man availeth much." (Jas. 5.16) "All of the fellow-members constitute one and the same body in Christ in the unity of the Spirit, and all ought to share with one another the benefit of the divine graces" – so comments St. Basil.[3] St. John Damascene gives the following synthesis of the tradition: "It is because of God that we venerate the saints, for they are his servants . . . friends of Christ, temples of the Spirit."

Thus the veneration of the saints is rooted in the Communion of Saints which transcends all limits of time and space. In the risen Christ the natural intercession of the living for the living finds this same entire freedom, leading on to the equally natural intercession of the saints, which is their manner of participating, in heaven, in the destiny of the Church on earth. We are surrounded by the protecting prayers of the saints. These prayers do not in the very least separate us from Christ but unite us to him more intimately. The saints are not "mediators" in the sense of diminishing the unique mediation of the Saviour; they are our friends and companions on the same path of salvation.

Indications in Holy Scripture, the Church's experience of the invoking of saints, their iconography, the dedication of churches to special saints chosen as guardians and protectors of individual neighbourhoods, the speedy circulation of their *Lives* – all these are different elements in the same tradition. The Church cultivates it attentively and regularises it by means of what is called the canonisation of saints.

[1] *P.G.* 12, 756.   [2] *P.L.* 2, 99.   [3] *De Spiritu Sancto, P.G.* 32, 180.

The canonisation of saints

Canonisation is nothing more than an official act of the Church in response to God's own judgement upon his saints. This judgement is expressed by means of various signs, and the ecclesiastical act merely establishes and records them.

Nectarius, Patriarch of Jerusalem (d. 1680), formulated the three conditions necessary for a canonisation:

1. Unquestionable orthodoxy of faith.
2. Holiness of life, and a confession of faith which would go as far as martyrdom if necessary.
3. Obvious manifestations of divine grace during lifetime or after death: miracles, healings, spiritual help, often but not always physical incorruptibility.

It must be stressed however that there are no precise rules or legal formalities to determine the procedure of canonisation, for it is something which evades all set rulings. There is a whole class of saints to whom the tradition does not ascribe any doings that are "supernatural" or miraculous in a specific sense. For example neither the Virgin nor St. John the Baptist – though "prototypes" of the ideal feminine and the ideal masculine – performed any miracles during their earthly lives. St. Vladimir, who was simply a Christian prince, brought baptism to the Russian people, and it was for this reason that he was canonised. The Council of 1547 canonised miracle-workers as well as martyrs, but in the case of Leontius, Bishop of Rostov (d. 1077), his hard apostleship alone justified his canonisation. The Church glorifies different categories of saints: patriarchs, prophets, martyrs, workers of miracles, theologians and Fathers of the Church, monks, ascetics, spiritual fathers, *anagyres*[1], princes, doctors, and pious laymen.

All ecstasies, visions and supernatural phenomena are considered as belonging to the novitiate. This is why a saint's life is always hidden, mysterious, steeped in humility and modesty; a great many saints remain unknown to the world – they are known only to God.

Miracles

All miracles testify to the existence of God and to his active presence in the world. Even people who regard religion as nothing more

---

[1] Physicians and wonder-workers who received no payment. [Ed.]

myth and who speak of the impossibility of miracles in this technological age – even these accept the reality of prayer. Yet prayer, though it is the most common form of faith, is at the same time its most enigmatic form, a "mystery" and a perpetual miracle.

God created the world, and it exists according to the laws of nature which he (the Creator) established. He has "laid the foundations of the earth, that it should not be removed for ever". (Ps. 104.5) Yet the world that God has created is a world in process of becoming; it is not static but dynamic. In the course of its evolution God the Creator gives way to God the Saviour, the God who says, "My Father worketh hitherto, and I work." Men, as higher beings, are created free. God enters into a relationship of interaction with man, making him open towards the energies of grace, but also open and creative towards the material universe. This is why, side by side with the natural determinism of necessity and of cause and effect in nature, there exists a spiritual process, the cause and effect of free creation.

Does a miracle suppress the natural course of events, whose sequence of cause and effect is so relentless? The drug a doctor introduces into a patient's organism, the suggestion of a psychiatrist, the intervention of a surgeon – any one of these may put a stop to the normal sequence of cause and effect in an illness which naturally leads towards death, by introducing a new cause whose effect is sufficiently strong to dominate and change the course of the illness, and so steer the patient towards recovery.

A believer can do this same thing by means of the healing influence of prayer and intercession, and this is in fact a miracle. In both instances we see a creative impetus acting upon nature by means of the introduction of a new factor; no matter whether it is a medical treatment or the energy of divine grace, it is a cross-current that changes the previous drift of inevitability, and directs the whole towards a new and different end. Natural laws are not violated but rather reformulated, one can even say they are "consummated", just as the Law, fulfilled by Christ, is made whole to the extent of becoming something quite different, namely grace.

No miracle is in any way supernatural, and above all it is not against nature; it is "supernaturally natural". The world is not a mechanism (like the deist's clock or the materialist's matter) but a living organism including both flesh and spirit, in which all can become spiritual, even the very flesh. Miracles, insofar as they are manifestations of power, can stem from opposite sources: "He that believeth on me, the works that I do shall he do also; and greater works than these shall he do", and at the other extreme "The working of Satan with all power and signs and lying wonders". (2 Thess. 2.9) Man, master of the universe, can show forth either the power of a prophet of God, the demoniacal power of one who practises witchcraft, or the art of a physician (who also demonstrates the creative genius of the human spirit). This is why all miracles demand a faith which is discerning. They are withheld from the super-stitious who misunderstand their causes, and also from the unhealthily curious, for no true miracle ever forces belief. A sense of awe preserves the mystery intact, and at the same time makes it astonishingly familiar, intimate, "supernaturally natural". It often causes surprise that the Orthodox seek for and find the mystical side of everything; indeed each situation that is encountered is overshadowed by the constant awareness of being everywhere with God and in his presence. This is a concept of existence essentially full of worship. He who accepts true miracles receives the power of the faith which can move mountains: "Give of thy blood and receive the Spirit."[1]

The miracles worked by Christ were always motivated by compassion and in response to faith, thus no violence was ever done to the laws of nature or to man's conscience. Christ performed his miracles as perfect Man, thus they are not beyond the power of human beings to whom divine grace has been given by God, and they belong to a dimension that is hidden even from nature. In his battle against sin, suffering and death, man can act either according to science, or by means of spiritual power, or by a combination of the two.

Christ's humanity was deified and that of a saint is also deified; thus every saint, but also every believer, is a "miracle-worker" — one who possesses spiritual power over nature and thereby redeems it.

The participation of the saints in life on earth

The saints, even after they have departed from us, continue in their own way to be effective members of the Church; they surround us with their prayers, and represent a living link between heaven and earth. As already said, they are not in any sense mediators and they do not in the least detract from the unique mission of the only Mediator who is Christ, but they help us as friends and elder brothers who have experience of the mysteries of God. Confidants of God's purpose and receptacles of

---

[1] A saying of Abbot Longinus. [Ed.]

grace, their intercession possesses great power by virtue of their intimate "relationship" with the holiness of God. In them the image of God has been consummated, and they have thereby become "very likenesses", each according to his own vocation and personal gifts. There are as many forms of sanctity as there are human personalities, and everyone can find his own individual version of it.

According to the faith of the Church, and also to its unfailing experience, God has granted to his saints the power of bringing active succour to men. They help us to unite ourselves before our heavenly Father. The man who is sensitive to this no longer feels lost in his solitude; he has a great family surrounding him, sustaining him, carrying him onward towards God.

In praying to the saints, we pray to Christ who is present within his saints; we address ourselves to that power of Christ's love which unites all within his Body. It is this indestructible communion between us all, and at the same time the organic unity of the spiritual and the bodily, which explains the cult of relics. The Church holds and affirms that there is a special link between the spirit of a saint and his remains (no matter whether they are intact or not) and that death does not destroy it. When our Lord's body was in the tomb his soul had been withdrawn from it – thus his death was real – but his body retained its link with the divine Spirit and by reason of this remained incorruptible. The same thing happens after the death of a saint. Because of their participation in the destiny of the living, the saints are given the grace of a continuing bond between spirit and body, a bond which is visibly manifested in their relics. This manner of being present is analogous to the presence manifested by means of their icons.

In the Eastern Liturgy (according to both St. John Chrysostom and St. Basil) a very special place is given to the saints. Through the Communion of Saints the glory of God shines out in his creatures. The Liturgy does not "teach" holiness, it does not in any sense explain the holiness of God, it is indeed incapable of doing so, but it reveals God's holiness, opens the doors before his coming and causes a powerful awareness of his presence. When, with incomparable art, it reaches one of its climaxes, a harmony of astonishing fulness prepares the way worthily for the coming of the Word.

"I say unto you, Hereafter ye shall see heaven open, and the angels of God ascending and descending upon the Son of man." (John 1.51) "And a voice came out of the throne, saying, Praise our God, all ye his servants." (Rev. 19.5) This moment of adoration, an essentially

L

liturgical act, reunites heaven and earth. When the priest pronounces the words "Blessed be the entrance of thy saints," this means that the outburst of praise to God is being shared by all the powers of sanctity that the Church possesses, by her very being. The fulness of the "cloud of witnesses" surrounding Christ (Heb. 12.1) irradiates the brilliance of the glory of God. The whole of the assembly of saints, with the angels and the faithful, together form the retinue of the King.

"O come, let us worship and fall down before Christ; Save us, O Son of God, who art wonderful in thy saints." While this is being chanted all the congregation prostrate themselves: God, the Holy that is hidden in the very mystery of his brightness, as in a cloud, advances, adored by all the powers of his own holiness which "shine from the faces of the saints". At the very heart of his transcendent holiness God, the Lover of mankind, brings about an overwhelming immanence by means of his coming amongst his saints. The glory of this holiness truly fills the temple, and it comes, as through the luminous fringes of a cloud, to lay its touch upon the congregation.

Struck by the blinding vision of heaven and earth, and overcome by this superabundance, the soul gives itself entirely, becomes pure offering, can do nothing but partake of the joyful utterance of the hymn to the blessed Trinity: "O Holy God, Holy and mighty, Holy immortal." Amid the fulness of the ceremonial adoration, Christ, Glory of the Holy, advances and appears before the faithful worshippers. It is from these heights that the benediction is given "Peace be to you all." Peace introduces the world into the company of the saints in anticipation of the Kingdom.

The veneration of the Theotokos, mother of God

In the eyes of the Fathers, the maternal function of the Church leads very naturally towards the veneration of the Virgin. For the Fathers, Mary was identified with Woman as the enemy of the Serpent, the woman clothed with the sun, the place of God's wisdom at its very source, which is integrity and chastity of being.

Just as the Holy Spirit represents divine holiness, so does the Virgin represent human holiness. The integrity of the virginal structure of her being triumphs over evil and possesses an invincible power. Linked by her very nature to the Holy Spirit, Mary thus appears as a bringer of life and consolation, a life-giving Eve who safeguards and protects every creature and thereby emerges as a symbol of the Church in her maternal and protective aspect. According to the Orthodox tradition, the dedication of the Virgin to the life of the Temple, and also her love of God, attained to such depth and intensity that the conception of the Son came about in her as the divine response to the deepening of her life of prayer and her transparency to the sanctifying energies of the Spirit.

Although the Virgin shared organically in the genealogical descent from Adam, and in the results of the Fall, she was nevertheless shielded from all personal impurity and from all evil. These were made harmless in her by means of the successive purifications of her ancestors, by the special action of the Spirit, and by her own free choice. This last factor, her willing response, is accentuated in a beautiful passage by Nicholas Cabasilas, the great fourteenth-century spiritual writer, which synthesises the teaching of the Fathers that man cannot be saved without the free consent of his own will: "The Incarnation was not only the work of the Father, of his goodness and his Spirit, but also the work of the will and faith of the Virgin. Without the consent of 'the most pure', without the cooperation of her faith, the plan was as impossible as without the intervention of the three divine Persons themselves. It was only after having instructed and persuaded her that God took her for his mother, and borrowed from her the flesh that she desired to lend to him. Just as he willingly became incarnate, so he wished that his mother should give birth to him of her own free choice."[1]

Orthodoxy asserts the perpetual virginity of the Theotokos[2]; it does not however accept the idea of "exemption" which is claimed by the Roman dogma of the Immaculate Conception. This dogma puts the Virgin apart, removes her from the common destiny of humanity, and implies a possibility of liberation from Original Sin prior to the Cross, in other words by grace alone. According to this the Redemption, in order to take place, would have had to exist already; the Virgin would have had to enjoy its effects before it actually came about. Such a purpose on the part of God, who had in the first place made Adam a righteous man entirely by means of grace, would, for Eastern Christians, make the Fall itself incomprehensible.

In the eyes of the ancient Greeks, man's "original goodness" was not a free gift but the very root of his being. God however does not act *upon* man but within him; he did not act upon the Virgin by a gift conferred

---

[1] *Homily on the Annunciation.*
[2] Icons of the Virgin show her wearing three stars, one on the head and one on each shoulder; these symbolise her virginity before, during and after the Nativity.

on her from outside. All good imposed from without becomes evil. Nothing except the willing submission of sanctity provides the objective human condition of the Incarnation that enables the Word to "come home". Grace never violates or forces the natural order but transcends it. Jesus was able to assume human flesh because it was given to him by humanity in the shape of Mary; through the Virgin all mankind can say "Yea, Lord, Come." That is why, for the Fathers, the phrase in the Creed "incarnate of the Holy Ghost and the Virgin Mary" had a second meaning, namely the mystery of the second birth of every believer who is born again of faith and of the Holy Spirit, for the faith of every believer is rooted in the universal validity of the Virgin's response, in other words of her *Fiat*. She was the first to fulfil the final purpose for which the world had been brought into being, "to be the frontier between the created and the uncreated"[1], and by means of her "the Trinity was glorified".[2] By giving birth to Christ, insofar as she is Eve, she gives birth to him on behalf of all, and so it is she who gives birth to him within every individual soul. The Church, thus, is represented in her function of "mystical matrix", of continual birth-giver, of everlasting Theotokos.

St. Maximus the Confessor defines a "mystic" as "he in whom the birth of the Saviour is most clearly manifest"; he also says that contemplation "makes the fruitful soul both virgin and mother at the same time".[3] On this same theme St. Ambrose writes, "Every believing soul conceives and gives birth to the Word of God; Christ, by means of our faith, is the fruit of us all, thus we are all mothers of Christ." [4] These words throw helpful light upon one of the sayings of Jesus, "My mother and my brethren are these which hear the word of God, and do it." (Luke 8.21) The emphasis is laid not upon the Virgin, but upon all men: "Whosoever shall do the will of my Father . . . the same is my mother . . . "; this text means that to all is granted the grace of giving birth to Christ in the soul.

The Orthodox feast of *Pokrov*, a feast which celebrates the protection and intercession of the Mother of God, gives a clear explanation of her ministry. The origin of the feast goes back to a vision that was shared by Andrew, a "fool in Christ", and his disciple Epiphanus. The vision took place at Constantinople, in the Church dedicated to the Virgin of Blachernæ. According to the testimony of these two witnesses the Virgin, kneeling, was weeping over the world, and begging her Son to

---

[1] St. Gregory Palamas, *P.G.* 151: 472B.   [2] St. Cyril of Alexandria, *P.G.* 78: 992.
[3] *P.G.* 90: 889c.   [4] *In Evang. S. Lucas*, II, 26.

grant it his pardon. At the end of her prayer the Virgin lifted her veil sparkling with light (*pokrov*) from off her head and stretched it out over all those present and indeed over the whole world as a sign of protection. The veil was like the heavens covering the earth. There is a fifteenth-century icon which shows an astonishing unity between the veil and the saints who are protected by it. One might almost say that the veil is woven of sanctity, forming a protective wall, a radiant shelter of salvation. This shining wall of witnesses discloses hands raised in supplication; the Church prays for the Church, but the hands of the Mother of God bear the burden of the entire universe.

Dionysius the Areopagite addressed a prayer to the Theotokos which well expresses her ministry. "I desire," he prayed, "that thy icon should be reflected ceaselessly in the mirror of souls, and that it should keep them pure until the end of all ages, that it should lift up those who are bent down towards the earth, that it should give hope and joy to all who venerate and follow after thy eternal beauty."

Training in sanctity: the art of the spiritual fathers

"Call no man your father upon the earth," said the Lord, "for one is your Father, which is in heaven." And yet, in the Eastern Church, since the earliest days of Christianity, we find references to "spiritual fathers" (or simply "fathers"), to elders, "simple old men", to "*startsi*"[1]. The evolution of the Jewish word *abba* is rich in meaning. It has found its way into every language, but since Old Testament times it has come to have an absolutely new meaning. This newness stems from the revelation of the Trinity. "Abba, Father", the words used in prayer by Jesus himself (Mark 14.36), express a degree of intimacy unthinkable in a Jewish prayer. The Gospel reveals the Father's love for the Son, a love which causes the divine fatherhood to flow forth upon all men, upon all God's children, and indeed the Lord himself taught us to say "Our Father". According to the *Epistle to Diognetus* the first stage in the initiation of catechumens[2] was for them to become familiar with their heavenly Father – Abba, Father – by means of the Son and of the Spirit. St. Cyril of Alexandria (in his *Thesaurus*) writes that in Christ the relationship of master and slave gives way to the mystery of Father and

[1] Plural of *starets*. A *starets* is a holy man, who is spiritually experienced and sought out intuitively by the people as a counsellor and guide because of his spiritual gifts. [Ed.]
[2] Early Christians undergoing instruction prior to baptism. [Ed.]

Son. It is this understanding of the Trinity that enables Orthodox tradition to find in the Gospel a justification for the practice of spiritual fatherhood: it is a rendering of homage to the unique divine fatherhood, which manifests itself by means of various different forms of human relationship. St. Pachomius was, according to *Les Vies Coptes de S. Pachôme*, "for his disciples, their father after God". It was in this sense that St. John wrote "my little children" and St. Paul spoke of enduring the pangs of childbirth. The art of fatherhood is not something to be learnt like a science at school. In the tradition of the ascetic fathers the verb "engender" is used to describe the transmission of graces.

The title "Father of the Church" (when used for the great doctors and theologians who are Fathers of the whole Church, in the context of true doctrine and dogma) must be understood as having a quite separate connotation. But as regards the title "Father", when it means a personal and spiritual relationship, there are two traditions: one of them goes back to St. Ignatius of Antioch and means an "ecclesiastical fatherhood"; all bishops and priests are called "Father" by reason of their priesthood. They baptise, they bring about the divine filiation by means of the sacraments, they exercise their pastoral gifts. The second tradition stems from the Desert Fathers. The paternity of such fathers has nothing to do with priestly functions. St. Anthony the Great, founder of monasticism, was a simple layman. Here a man becomes a "father" from a divine choice, by virtue of special grace from the Holy Spirit and by reason of being called to a divine discipleship, which means being taught directly by God. Neither age nor status has any bearing on this. As shown in their *Lives*, these men of God became Abba or Father to such an extent that the collections of their sayings and deeds have become accepted as belonging to the *Apophthegmata Patrum*. How significant it is that bishops came for help and counsel to these simple folk, these monks or laymen who were directly guided by the Holy Spirit. The common people never failed to recognise them, and their charismatic ministry was accepted as existing within the ordinary realm of episcopal authority.

The heart illumined by understanding and the mind orientated by a thirst for the divine open themselves up to the Spirit. The essential condition for becoming a "spiritual father" is to have become first of all *pneumatikos*, "spiritual", oneself. St. Simeon the New Theologian wrote of it thus: "He who has not yet been reborn is not capable of giving birth to spiritual children," and he also adds, "The Spirit, to be imparted, must firstly, be received." To attain to this state there must initially be a healing of the breach between the dynamic function of the heart and the cognitive function of the intelligence. Hesychasm (the tradition of the silent contemplatives) re-establishes, above all, this integrity of the human being. It makes the spirit, or intellect, "come down into the heart".[1]

Spiritual fatherhood is not a formal ministry but one of life and being. St. Gregory Palamas insists on this: "Our piety," he says, "consists of realities and not of words." Among the graces of a "father" the foremost is love or charity, and its surest mark is martyrdom, either visible to the world or hidden from it. "No asceticism" — so assert the great spiritual writers — "if lacking in charity, if less than 'a sacrament of brotherly love', comes anywhere near to God." According to St. Gregory of Nazianzus, "A man who is truly spiritual is a repository of divine love for mankind." "His heart burns with love for every creature, even for reptiles and demons," so wrote St. Isaac, thus describing the "ontological tenderness" which is the universal love of the saints. Abbot Poemen refused to give punishments, and in his position as father he showed a motherly tenderness: "When I see one of the brothers getting drowsy during the Divine Office, I put his head on my knees and let him rest."

Another grace sometimes bestowed on a father is "the prayer of flame", when all self-awareness is lost. St. Isaac and many others while in prayer saw "the fire of all things" and were themselves transformed into columns of light. "If thou wouldst be perfect, become wholly fire," so said Abba Joseph.

Then there is also the gift of prophecy, the deciphering of God's purpose in individual cases, the spiritual knowledge of men's hearts, the understanding of their secret thoughts, the discernment of spirits and the gift of insight. The fathers could read souls, could tell the contents of a letter without opening it, and above all were able to bring men's hearts out of hiding. Long before the discoveries of modern depth psychology, they were masters of the amazing art of penetrating the subconscious. "Many passions are hidden in our souls, though they entirely escape attention. Temptation shows them up." And again: "He who expresses his thoughts is quickly healed; he who hides them makes himself ill." "Bring your thoughts to light, seek the counsel of a father who is able to detect them."

[1] This "prayer of the heart" or "Jesus prayer" is based on the prayer of the publican. (Luke 18:13). [Ed.]

The terrible sin of pride – *philautia* – shuts man up in himself. In order to fight it, as well as the domination of the passions and the spirit of self-sufficiency, all novices are trained in obedience. The fathers taught this obedience by the example of their own lives, and obtained it by unceasing prayer.

The final stage of sonship, however, transcends obedience, and this transcending means that the human will is entirely replaced by the divine will. Here one comes to the essential purpose of spiritual fatherhood: its sole aim is to lead the way from the state of slavery to the freedom of the children of God.

This is why the Fathers give constant warnings against the dangers and risks of seeking for a spiritual counsellor. St. Basil advises finding a "friend of God", one in whom, beyond any doubt, God himself speaks. The greater a father's authority, the greater his self-effacement. St. Serafim of Sarov defines the spiritual father's art as follows: "I entirely disregard my own will and my own knowledge of souls; I listen to the promptings of the Spirit."

According to Abbot Poemen, a father puts a soul into direct relationship with God, and he adds this advice: "Never give orders; be an example to all but never a lawgiver." It is not in conformity to rules, but in God, that the path is taken together. The fear of violating the personal integrity of the disciple explains the father's entire oblation of himself.

A spiritual father is never a "director of conscience". He never gives birth to his own spiritual child but to a child of God who is adult and free. Both of them, together, make themselves learners in the school of Truth. The disciple receives the grace of spiritual attention, the father receives the grace of being a channel of the Holy Spirit. All obedience here is obedience to the will of the heavenly Father, and at the same time a participation in the acts of the obedient Christ.

There must be no subservience to human influence, no idolatry of a father, even if he is a saint. All counsel given by a father leads towards a state of liberation, of worship before the face of God. True obedience crucifies all self-will in order to bring to life the supreme freedom, the human spirit attuned and open to the Holy Spirit.

The most profound message of the Fathers for our times is the appeal for a return of the human heart to the restoring liberty of the divine heart. The sanctity of a man who has been "born again" is a creative and daring holiness: "Light dwells within a man of light, and he illumines the whole world."

Typical examples of Russian holiness

Once a nation has been converted to Christianity, it can never be passive as regards the way it receives, assimilates and lives its faith. In a sense the national genius imparts a personality of its own to the universal tradition. The religious life of a people, as it is lived through the centuries, gives shape to a religious ideal in which the popular beliefs and aspirations are synthesised. This ideal shows itself in doctrines and ideas as well as in forms of worship and piety, but it is most clearly evident in a country's saints; they are like living icons of the national spirituality.

In Russia the most striking features of the religious ideal are its remarkable balance and absence of excess. There is no such thing in the Russian tradition as an asceticism of pure mortification; even the very term "asceticism" is unfamiliar, although its meaning is expressed by three very simple words: fasting, work, and prayer. The flame of spirituality has always been kept alight in the monasteries, which on a practical level have justified their existence by means of their ministry to the people. The priest-monks have always given themselves to hospitality and good works as a condition of the spiritual growth of their communities.

Sanctity has come to express more and more the Russian people's love for the self-giving Christ, the humble, simple Christ who always stoops to meet the poor, the humiliated and the suffering. In the twentieth century the Russian painter Nesterov gave shape to this merciful aspect of Christ's radiance in his celebrated picture "Holy Russia". Dostoïevsky says: "Perhaps the supreme devotion of the Russian people is towards the merciful Christ, whose special kind of love is a suffering love."

This has always been so: the first Russian saints to be canonised, the holy princes Boris and Gleb, represent a very special class of those innocents who share in the Passion and freely accept a violent death without any resistance. They symbolise the pure and innocent Lamb, sacrificed as an oblation. Furthermore although a few *startsi* and "fools in Christ" are to be found everywhere, in Russia they have, perhaps, been very specially loved and sought after.

No one saint ever expresses the whole of the spirituality from which he has sprung; he is merely one of its rays. Nevertheless he has been begotten by the spirituality of his own Church, and therefore one can distinguish through him some of its essential features. St. Serafim of

Sarov revives the experience of the great spiritual masters – St. Macarius of Egypt, St. Simeon the New Theologian, St. Gregory Palamas – yet he also represents a synthesis of Russian sanctity. His radiant face, his life, his teaching, take one to the very heart of Orthodoxy. Furthermore his paschal joy is not merely a characteristic of his personal temperament; it reveals the essence of the Eastern tradition. But his white robes, his joy, his prophecies, point towards a new age, very possibly towards the eve of the Apocalypse. On his feast day the following sentence from the Acathistus Hymn is sung: "Rejoice with the joy of the Kingdom which thou hast already tasted upon earth."

The life of St. Serafim of Sarov

St. Serafim of Sarov lived from 1759 to 1833. A contemporary of Pushkin's, he died when Gogol was twenty-four and Dostoïevsky twelve. Outwardly the course of his life was very simple but it was marked throughout by continual signs of divine power; miraculous healings, apparitions of the Virgin and prophecies were part of his life. Tall and strong, with a lively and intelligent demeanour, already well versed in the Scriptures and in the writings of the Fathers of the Church, possessed of a radiant spiritual beauty, he became a novice in the monastery o Sarov at nineteen; when he was twenty-seven he took monastic vows and received the name of Serafim.

After eight years he withdrew into the forest to live the life of a hermit. He longed to be alone with God. "I could hardly believe I was living on the earth, my soul was so full of joy," he later said. Joy in such circumstances is rare – astonishing even; several monks had tried living in the same vicinity, in the heart of the forest, but not one had been able to bear the rigours of the austere life. He shared his daily ration of bread with the wild beasts, who waited patiently for his return. "How do you manage to have enough for them all?" he was asked. "I have no idea," replied the saint. "God alone knows how."

During the years he spent in isolation and complete solitude St. Serafim suffered a terrible spiritual conflict; in his own words: "He who has chosen the desert and silence must feel himself constantly crucified." He established himself on a rock in the depths of the forest, and there for three years prayed the Jesus prayer without ceasing. During this period he himself became living, incarnate prayer, but only at the end of it did a divine peace flow into his soul.

One day, having been beaten almost to death by brigands, St.

Serafim was visited by the Virgin accompanied by the apostles Peter and John. When she had healed him she said to the Apostles: "This man is one of us." But although he recovered Serafim remained a cripple and always walked with a stick, while his hair had turned completely white. When the brigands were arrested, the saint begged for them to be pardoned, and threatened to leave the district if they were not. After this episode however he left the forest and returned to the world of men. For five years he lived in the monastery, enclosed and solitary. Then, in obedience to a command from the Virgin, he relaxed his rule of solitude and enclosure, and set the door of his cell ajar. People flocked to it just to hear the sound of his voice.

After thirty-seven years of monastic life St. Serafim now re-entered the world and began his ministry as a *starets*. In this essentially charismatic ministry his outstanding gifts were as healer, confessor and prophet. As a healer he quoted the command: "Heal the sick . . . cast out devils", and he believed that his special gift of healing was an expression of his priesthood. As confessor he used to say to young priests: "Always remember that you are no more than witnesses, God alone acts." Taking upon himself the sins of others, he would prostrate himself beside a penitent telling him to pray to the Lord for his [Serafim's] sins. Thus he showed how the Communion of Saints participates in sin, and how guilt is shared by all alike. Not interested in lists of shortcomings, since what he perceived was the whole man, he sought to find humility and faith in a penitent's heart. As prophet he was always pronouncing warnings. To be a prophet is not only to predict the future; above all it is to be a messenger of God's judgement: "We are drawing down God's wrath upon ourselves," he would cry in deep anguish. He spoke of the time when Antichrist would begin to despoil the churches and destroy the monasteries. "It will be a sorrow such as has never been since the beginning of the world." He predicted many of the events of the Russian revolution.

In 1831, on the eve of the Annunciation, the Virgin appeared to St. Serafim for the twelfth and last time. A nun shared with him in the joy of the vision, and afterwards gave a description of it. The Virgin had come to forewarn the saint: "Soon, my friend, you will be with us." "What joy awaits the soul when the angels come to seek it," he replied, radiant and full of joy to have reached this final stage. On New Year's Day 1833, a Sunday, the saint made his communion, then bade fare-well to all the brothers who were present. In the evening he was heard chanting Easter anthems, despite the inappropriateness of the season.

Next morning he was found on his knees before the icon of the Virgin which is known as "the joy of all joys". His hands were crossed on his breast and his eyes were closed.

"For us, dying will be a joy," he had explained to a nun who was distressed by the idea of death. The usual greeting which the saint had been wont to give to everyone he met was: "My joy, Christ is risen." It conveys a permanent quality of his soul, an all-abiding paschal exultation that colours everything with its light.

St. Serafim had above all been a *starets*. He devoted himself to the ministry of consolation. "Visit the fatherless and widows in their affliction." The comforting of such afflicted as these was the foremost object of his priesthood. Even in a crowd he could immediately pick out the "afflicted", the despairing, the cast down. There is a kind of sorrow which is a sin against the Holy Spirit. In the philosophy of despair, so widespread at the present time, life itself is portrayed in terms of anxieties. Yet according to those who understand the things of the spirit, all anxieties stem from the agonised anticipation of death by one who fails, now here on earth, to share in the "little resurrection" – the essential grace of the sacrament of baptism.

As St. Serafim came into touch with the afflicted, he brought his peace to their souls. Suffering, in the Eastern tradition, is not sought after for its own sake, either as a means of acquiring merit or for the expiation of sin; it is regarded simply as a means of purification in order to attain to joy. The eschatological atmosphere of the first centuries, with their expectation of the Kingdom, came to life again in Serafim, and he taught how to "die joyfully". "A living peace and lightheartedness" are the signs of the Holy Spirit's presence, "for wherever God dwells he creates joy".

The concept of salvation as healing

St. Serafim was often gravely ill and each time he was miraculously cured by the intervention of the Virgin. He declined all medical help but begged everyone to pray for him more intensely. When, after one illness lasting three years, he finally recovered, he started to collect funds to build a chapel for the infirmary of the near-by convent. This chapel was to be the visible sign of a spiritual place of healing under the direction of God himself. In the saint's own words: "He alone is the healer of both souls and bodies." He constantly repeated the prayer which accompanies Communion: "[That] the partaking of thy holy

mysteries . . . O Lord [may be] unto the healing of my soul and body."
This illustrates the therapeutic concept of the sacraments in the Eastern
tradition. The priest who hears a confession does not want to impose
punishments; he seeks for new conditions in which the sick penitent will
not be exposed to temptation. This is expressed in the prayer preceding
confession: "You have come to the physician, do not then leave him
without being healed." Similarly the Trullan Synod (692) decreed:
"Confessors should behave like doctors who are eager to find the
remedy each penitent needs." Even the canon laws should be used by a
bishop as "healing ordinances."

When he was healing Manturov, a desperately sick man, St. Serafim
said to him, "By the grace which is given to me, I treat your sickness",
and he added: "It is not for me to give life or death, to lead into hell or
out of it. These things are in the hands of the one Saviour who hearkens
to prayer."

Sinners are suffering from a fatal disease and for them life is already
hell. But repentance and faith immediately bring about the conditions
needed for recovery, they bring the soul out of hell and place it on the
threshold of the Kingdom. It is true that even repentance and faith are
gifts which are sown by the Spirit, but they cannot germinate except in
the ground of humility. Humility is not a weakness but the most immense
power, for it shifts the axis of being from the ego to God. Ascetics regard humility as the art of finding oneself in one's true place. It is the
attitude of the handmaid of the Lord and the friend of the Bridegroom. The healing which is salvation restores order, beauty, universal
harmony. *Philokalia*, the Greek title of a collection of ascetic writings,
means love of the beautiful.[1] A saint is good, but he is also full of an
inner beauty and harmony. In him human life resembles a liturgical
office; it is comparable to the architecture of a temple or to an icon,
for it teaches the art of "entering into the very likeness" of the Kingdom.

St. Serafim's life of prayer and the theology of prayer

The patristic axiom that "the theologian is he who knows how to
pray" explains very well one of the two meanings of the word "Orthodoxy": it means "right worship" as well as "right doctrine". True
theology is always a form of prayer; it translates the direct experience of

---

[1] The Russian text is known as *Dobrotolubiye*. The English translation of some of these
writings is published by Faber and Faber. [Ed.]

God, the experience which unites, into theological language. This is why the Fathers read the Bible as though they were receiving the Eucharistic gifts; they sought, above all, the presence of Christ and communion with him.

St. Serafim, when he read the Holy Scriptures or the writings of the Fathers, meditated in prayer on the texts, standing as in vigil. He always read standing upright before an icon, as though saying the Divine Office. Once when he spoke to a novice on the subject of St. Paul's rapture it was clear that he himself was sharing the same experience. Stooping, and with his eyes closed, he seemed to be perceiving and listening with deep and ever-fresh astonishment; then he spoke: "If you only knew what joy awaits our souls in heaven. But if even St. Paul found no words to express it, who then can speak of it?" This is why, so he liked to say, "It is good to speak of God, but it is better still to make oneself pure for him." In the Divine Office of the Orthodox Church theology is expounded but it is also prayed and lived. Such theology is not an intellectual system, but an assimilation of the spirit of the Fathers, and thereby of the spirit of the Apostles. Through St. John Climacus, St. Macarius, St. Simeon, St. Gregory Palamas or St. Serafim we ourselves can lay hold of the same source, the Apostles themselves.

In his life of prayer St. Serafim followed the ancient rule of St. Pachomius of Egypt. But in his practice of the "prayer of the heart" or "Jesus prayer" he was chiefly a follower of Nil Sorsky. This prayer frees the heart from distractions and draws Jesus into it by means of the unceasing invocation: "Lord Jesus Christ, Son of God, have mercy on me, a sinner." (Luke 18.13) It eliminates all discursiveness and in time becomes a single word, the name of Jesus. The holy name echoes continually in the depths of the soul and in some way "adheres" to the breathing – the breath of life that links body and soul together. This is an inner equivalent of the Eucharist, an unending communion with Jesus who is present in his name. When Jesus has been drawn into the heart, the Kingdom has come and the soul is at peace, hence the expression "hesychasm" which means tranquillity. It was in the context of this prayer that St. Serafim replied when he was asked about a choice between the contemplative life and the active life: "Acquire inner peace, and a multitude of men will find their salvation beside you."

The name of Jesus, repeated ceaselessly, merges into his presence, and in this presence man is transformed. In terms of iconography this is shown by the haloes of the saints; the luminosity of their bodies is a normal feature of their being. It also signifies the state of the new creature.

St. Serafim's teaching on the Holy Spirit

A strong leaning towards the theology of the Holy Spirit, inherent in the monasticism of the Eastern Church, links St. Serafim with St. Simeon the New Theologian and St. Tikhon of Zadonsk; all of them were prophets and heralds of the joy of the age to come.

Affinity with the Holy Spirit is at the heart of St. Serafim's asceticism, which was extreme in form and striking in its joy. Every soul that is crucified in Christ, said the saint, calls to the Holy Spirit: "O God give us thy peace." Every soul is brought to life by the Holy Spirit so that it may be illumined by the holy mystery of the Three in One." This life-giving power of the Holy Spirit explains the meaning of the Ortho- dox doctrine of *theosis* – the infusion of the Spirit, the penetration of the entire human being by the divine energies. Fasting and penance form the horizontal lines of purification ("Cleanse us from all impurity") while prayer, in the sense of conscious communion, is vertical; it is the flame of the consuming nearness of God ("Come and dwell in us"). "God is a fire which inflames our hearts with perfect love for him and for our neighbour." Thus every man who is truly spiritual "adds fire to fire".

St. Serafim often quoted the text: "My son, give me thine heart" (Prov. 23.26) "and I will give thee all besides", and the corresponding saying in the Gospels: "Seek ye first the kingdom of God . . . and all these things shall be added unto you." These texts show that the offering of the human heart to God, and the gift of the Kingdom of heaven to man, are complementary to one another, and that their coincidence represents the purpose of divine creation. The variation of the Lord's Prayer which renders "Thy Kingdom come" as "Thy Spirit come" identifies the coming of the Kingdom with the coming of the Holy Spirit. It is in the offering of the heart to God that the Spirit is manifested, thereby introducing the human being into the eternal exchange of love between the Father and the Son – which mutual self-giving is, in fact, the Kingdom. In the light of this we can understand St. Serafim's definition of the aim of Christian life: the acquiring of the Spirit's gifts as well as the receiving of the Holy Spirit.

According to an axiom of the Fathers "God cannot force anyone to love Him". This means that the offering of the heart to God is the supreme expression of human freedom. The heart is like an open space – St. Macarius spoke of "the open pastures of the heart" wherein the human spirit can breathe deep of the Holy Spirit, until at last it too "bloweth where it listeth". Thus it becomes an icon of the Spirit – a place of the living presence of God.

St. Serafim's theology of the Holy Spirit has a bearing upon the philosophy of history, and upon the meaning of existence in time. The inherent conditions of the temporal, with their potentiality for change, evolution, growth, mean that there can be an increase, a development, of the state of grace, a transmutation into fire and light. According to St. Serafim, the parable of the ten virgins shows that although the foolish virgins were moral beings (since they were virgins), dedicated and full of virtues, their empty lamps symbolise the sterility of their efforts because of their failure to recognise the one thing needful. The springs of grace, the gifts of the Holy Spirit, had been dried up within them.

The revelations of St. Serafim. The conversation with Motovilov

The revelations of St. Serafim bring to life again, in our own day, the heart of the experience of the Desert Fathers. He perceived, at a stage of the evolution of thought characterised by complexity and disintegration, that the norm of true simplicity was rapidly being lost, and he commented upon it thus: "Some passages of Holy Scripture seem foreign to us today. We ask whether one can admit that men are able to see God in the definite way described there. We are separating ourselves from the primitive simplicity of Christian knowledge. Under pretence of being 'enlightened' we have entered such a darkness of ignorance that today we regard all such things as inconceivable, though they were clear enough to people in the past, and enabled them to speak of God's manifestations to men as of things that were well known to all, and not in the least strange." It is very important that this warning should be heeded before we go on to the story of the conversation with Motovilov.

The saint's questioner, Motovilov, was one of his closest disciples, who had been miraculously healed of paralysis of the legs. The conversation took place in the heart of the forest, during the winter of 1831. St. Serafim began by explaining that the purpose of life was the acquiring of the Holy Spirit. Motovilov asked for further details about the state of grace. The saint told him to look at him. "I gazed, and was filled with awe," Motovilov later recounted. The saint appeared to be clothed with the sun. Asked what he felt, Motovilov replied that he was experiencing "an ineffable joy, as well as complete calm and peace". In addition to this harmony of soul there were external signs perceptible to the senses: a dazzling radiance and an unaccustomed feeling of warmth and fragrance. The saint then ended the conversation with these words: "It is not only to you that the understanding of these things is given, but through you to the whole world." Here then is a very important revelation, and a message addressed to all.

The experience thus described was not an ecstasy but a glimpse, in advance, of the transfiguration of man's entire being. One of its most striking features is the participation of the senses. Grace that is experienced, lived, and felt as sweetness, peace, joy and light, is a foreshadowing of the state of being of the age to come. It is not a matter of suppressing senses disorientated by the fall, nor of their replacement by new receptive organs, but of their transfiguration; they are lifted up to their original state. "The body itself shares in the process of sanctification."

Both the spiritual and bodily aspects of man are affected by the historic facts of the Incarnation and Redemption, and the Kingdom of God reveals itself in advance, by means of grace, in the whole of a human being. In Orthodox worship the use of chanting that is heard, icons that are contemplated, incense that is breathed, as well as the tangible elements which are partaken of in the Eucharist, make it possible to speak of liturgical sight, hearing, smell and taste. Matter is lifted up to the level of its own transcendent perfection, thus showing that it is not an autonomous or neutral substance, but an instrument of the Spirit and a vehicle of the spiritual.

The use of icons in worship leads to the habit of perceiving that material things are overflowing with the light and glory of God, and of grasping in them the fire which is at the heart of all. Ascetic purification and "visual abstinence" uplift the senses without ever leading to mere aesthetics or to abstraction. Matter is a vehicle for the divine energies, and it leads the eye towards the light of Tabor. "In the Transfiguration," says St. John Damascene, "Christ appeared to his disciples as he truly was, by opening their eyes." St. Gregory Palamas explains this further: "Light was not only the object of the vision, but also the means of beholding it."

During his conversation with Motovilov, St. Serafim himself conveyed this same point: "You too have become as full of light as I am . . .

M

If not you would not be able to see me thus." "Those who are worthy," says St. Gregory Palamas, "receive the necessary grace, and perceive by means of the senses as well as by the understanding that which is entirely beyond both senses and intellect." Thus by virtue of man's asceticism matter is restored to its place as the basis, the flesh, of the Resurrection. Even though transcendent, the uncreated divine light reveals itself to man in his wholeness. The paradox remains: the divine light is neither material nor accessible to the senses or mind, but it gives itself and lends itself to the contemplation of the eyes of one whose body has been transfigured. God makes himself known to the man who has been "born again" and whose whole existence has been recreated in Christ. This experience is not at all the same thing as the mysticism of the Messalians [1] nor is it a reduction of the divine fulness to the only level man can understand, nor is it a gross materialisation of the spiritual; it is communion between the created nature of the whole man and the uncreated God.

It is the "mystery of the eighth day", whose reality comes into being in the sacraments and is foreshadowed in the experience of the saints. As St. Serafim says, the "breath of life" which was Adam's Pentecost, the lights of Tabor, of the apostles' Pentecost itself, and of the sacramental Pentecost, the light that shines through the Liturgy, and the light of the Second Coming, are all of them one and the same. It is very important to grasp this so as to understand all the dimensions of Orthodox spirituality.

This spirituality is rooted in the fact of the Incarnation in its fullest sense, for it is concerned not only with the whole man but also with the universe which is under man's domination and which shares in his resurrection. It emphasises what one might call the real, or materialised, aspect of the Kingdom of God, whose beauty already shows itself in the forms of this world – the world which is being prepared to become the Kingdom.

It showed itself in a vision which was granted to St. Serafim when he was a deacon; he saw Christ himself, surrounded by angels, taking part in the Liturgy. And when after the Liturgy, he distributed the bread that remained, he was handing on the visible fruits of the "new earth", the very fruits of heaven. Furthermore in the accounts of his visions of the Virgin and of the apostles and saints there are innumerable details which are historically accurate, showing very clearly that there was no question of any adaptation of the spiritual to gross human sense; the

---

[1] A sect condemned by the Council of Ephesus A.D. 431. [Ed.]

senses in their entirety, along with the whole material plane, were uplifted to the spiritual level. This follows the very definite pattern of the manifestations of deity to man described in the Bible.

Such teaching is most illuminating, and it explains the localised presence of the spiritual in places of pilgrimage and other similar shrines; it also explains the possibility of communion with departed saints, who live on in their names, and in certain places such as their tombs, as well as in their relics. The saints have a special link with life on earth and never entirely leave it; they possess the gift of responding and of being present whenever their names are spoken in prayer. The name, the place, the relics; any of these can become the focal point of a spiritual presence. St. Serafim used to recall the words of our Lord: "I will not leave you comfortless: I will come to you" (John 14.18), and before his death he assured his disciples, "I shall still be alive . . . come to my tomb and open your soul to me . . . speak of me as one who is still living." Death and separation are thus truly transcended; this world and the other become amazingly close, and God gives to all men the chance to share in this greatest of intimacies and this spontaneous freedom.

Father John of Kronstadt

On the eve of the Russian revolution there arose the radiant figure of Father John of Kronstadt (1829-1908). Even beyond Russia he was famed for his powers as a healer; those who wrote to him asking for his prayers (and who subsequently received the desired healing) included the non-Orthodox – even Moslems. His spirituality was rooted in the practice of the Jesus prayer.[1] "So as to resist the continual onslaught of temptation," he said, "the Jesus prayer must be kept alive in the heart."

Though he was a married priest, his main work, *My Life in Christ*, recalls the treatise by the great fourteenth-century layman Nicholas Cabasilas, *Concerning the Life in Jesus Christ*. He held that the Eucharist was the source of his exceptional graces and said of it, "When I do not celebrate the Liturgy . . . I die . . . There infinite Love reveals itself . . . Thou art there in thy fulness. There we see thee, touch thee, feel thee."

A spiritual descendant of St. Serafim of Sarov, he brought to life the words of St. Paul: "Not I, but Christ liveth in me." By means of his intercession he became the priest of the Russian people on the eve of

---

[1] "Lord Jesus Christ, Son of God, have mercy on me, a sinner." [Ed.]

their greatest tribulations.[1] He was a prophetic sign, a vessel of the gifts of the Holy Spirit, a light for his time – by virtue of his simplicity, transparency and amazing power. He was all fire: a pentecostal flame, a blazing witness of the Love that is crucified for all human beings.

The ultimate message

It is clear that the great figures among the monks transcend their own monastic state, as indeed they transcend all rules and set forms. St. Serafim, at the decisive moment of his ministry, abandoned the extreme life of hermit and stylite, and returned to the world. It seems that having acquired the Holy Spirit he was called to a state beyond even monasticism. In a sense he was no longer a monk withdrawn from the world, nor was he a man living in the world; he was at the same time both of these and also something far greater: he had become the disciple, witness and confidant of the Holy Spirit. To Motovilov he said, "As to the fact that you are a layman and I am a monk, there is no need to give it a thought . . . The Lord seeks for hearts full of love towards God and one's neighbour . . . He hearkens just as much to the prayers of a monk as to those of a simple layman, provided they both have true faith, are genuine believers, and love God from the bottom of their hearts. Both of them will move mountains." The monk and the layman, both of them, stand as symbols of the "wholly other" and pointers towards it; they are witnesses to the Last Things; both are disciples of the Holy Spirit. Monks leave the world so that eventually they may find it again, surmounting every state, every static form, and "coming of age in Christ". The layman, on his side, is also called to transcend his own state, in the direction of interior monasticism, with the practical equivalent of the three monastic vows. These three vows represent a great charter of human liberty: poverty frees man from the domination of the material and is the baptismal transformation of the new creature; chastity frees from the domination of the carnal and is the nuptial mystery of *agape*[2]; obedience liberates from the idolatrous domination of the ego, and is the equivalent of being newly begotten of the Father. All men, whether monks or not, pray for these gifts as they follow the threefold pattern of the Lord's Prayer: exclusive obedience to the will of the Father, the poverty of one who hungers only for the

---

[1] Wars and the Revolution during this century. [Ed.]

[2] This term for Christian love originated from the Greek word *agape*, a love-feast connected with the Lord's supper. Later it became known as a fellowship meal. [Ed.]

eucharistic bread of eternity, and finally chastity, which is purification from the power of the Evil One.

The Gospel account of our Lord's three temptations in the wilderness shows the same theme in a striking way: Satan advocates the triple enslavement of man by means of miracles, magic, and absolute power. Christ, in his immortal answers, defines the triple liberation of man through poverty, chastity and obedience. Whether or not Constantine's empire drew secret strength from Satan's three temptations, monasticism was clearly based upon Christ's three answers, which indeed are reaffirmed in the three monastic vows. Such was the spirit of the first Desert Fathers, before there was any organisation of communities obeying a monastic rule. Those who knew how to derive grace from it responded to the genuine greatness of monasticism; above the institution, above all the distortions of history, the monastic state remains essentially, for every monk, a spiritual way of life. The layman, as a member of the universal priesthood, and insofar as he is a monk in his interior life, is also a man who is royally, absolutely free, and completely, entirely consecrated to his priesthood in the service of the Lord and the Church. Here perhaps is the essential message of St. Serafim, of the tradition of the Eastern Church, the message for everyone at the present day: the adult liberty of the child of God must be rediscovered, man must become a symbol of the Kingdom and go joyfully forward to meet the light of the Second Coming.

Conclusion: holiness today

Nowadays the very mention of holiness raises a psychological barrier. One thinks immediately of those giants of long ago, the hermits and the stylites, hidden in their caves or perched on their columns, but in such a way that these "illuminati", these "equals of the angels", seem no longer of this world. Sanctity seems out of date, as though it belonged to a past which has become alien and irrelevant to the disrupted patterns and syncopated rhythm of modern life. A saint is regarded merely as a kind of yogi, or more harshly as one who is ill, maladjusted, and in any case a useless creature. This attitude consigns sanctity to the cloister, far from the world of men, as something that is unusable, cumbersome, and good for nothing except to be stowed away in the depositories of history.

But history teaches us that different forms of witness supersede one another. Long ago martyrdom gave way to the monastic movement. The latter will retain its worth until the end of time, but its present critical condition is giving rise to the development of a special kind of response within the universal priesthood of the laity. Witness to the Christian faith in the setting of the modern world demands a universal vocation of interior monasticism for all believers, and it is this which gives shape to the new forms of sanctity.

According to the great masters, monks are none other than those who "desire to be saved", those who "live their lives according to the Gospel", who "seek for the one thing needful", who "in everything do violence to their own self-will". But these phrases also define precisely the ethic of all lay believers. The layman just as much as the monk himself stands as a signpost towards the "wholly other".

Monasticism, entirely centred upon the Last Things[1], once changed the face of the world. Today it makes its call to everyone, to laymen as well as to monks, and it represents a universal vocation. Everyone, whether celibate or married, finds his own personal way to it, his own personal equivalent of the monastic vows.

This vocation is not in any way an expression of a romantic mysticism; it is obedience to the Gospel in its most direct and realistic sense. Nor is it confined to great saints or the specially chosen. Even miracles are within the reach of our faith. The call of God, whose power fulfils itself in our weakness, comes to me and to each one of us. Kierkegaard wrote with deep insight: "One must read the Bible as a young man reads a letter from his beloved: it is written *for me*."

The possibility of becoming a new creature or a saint depends upon an immediate and firm decision in one's own mind and faith; one says yes, quite simply and humbly, and follows Christ with joy; then flowers bloom and miracles take place as a matter of course.

Throughout the tradition of the Fathers one can distinguish the type of layman who, in general, responds to the form of sanctity which is appropriate to him. He is above all a man of prayer, a being full of worship, who can sum up the whole of his life in the words of the psalmist: "I will sing praise to my God while I have my being." Such a layman is also a man who is freed by faith from "the great fear of the twentieth century" — fear of the bomb, of cancer, communism, death — whose faith always consists of loving the world in a special way, an extreme way of following the Lord, even as far as the descent into hell. Admittedly there is no theological doctrine concerning this, but perhaps it is only from the depths of hell that a hope overflowing with joy can come to life.

---

[1] Eschatology: death, last judgement, the state after death. [Ed.]

In Marxist countries, under tragic conditions of the most extreme tension, the Church teaches above all how to pray, how to take part in the fight by means of a silent witness, how to "listen to the silence of the Word" so as to give it a power transcending all the words of compromise. She exhorts the faithful to become temples, to make their whole lives an act of praise and worship, to turn a smiling countenance towards the men who have no faith. In the climate of silence and martyrdom of these oppressed countries an astonishing stream of prayer, a splendid doxology, circulates amongst the believers and calls us to "console the Consoler" by our love and abandonment to him: "Pardon us all, bless us all, thieves and Samaritans, those who fall on the road, and the priests who pass by on the other side; bless and pardon all our neighbours, the torturers and the victims, those who curse and those who are cursed by them, those who rebel against thee and those who bow in adoration before thy love. Take us all unto thee, Holy and righteous Father." In the immense cathedral which is God's universe, man, priest of his own life — no matter whether he is workman or thinker — makes of all humanity an offering, a hymn of praise to the Holy Trinity.

Christianity, in the greatness of its martyrs, in the royal dignity of all believers, is messianic, revolutionary, explosive. Within the kingdom of Caesar we are commanded to seek, and thus to find, that which does not belong there: the Kingdom of God. This command surely means that we must transform the shape of the world, must change its face, so that it becomes the dwelling place of the Kingdom.

One of the sure signs of the approach of the Kingdom is the longing for unity in the Christian world. While awaiting the end of all things, a hope, the great Christian hope, has come to life. As the prayers of the Churches arise they give form and shape to an "ecumenical epiclesis" invoking the descent of the Holy Spirit, so that the miracle of unity may come to pass. This is the ardent desire, the ardent prayer, of all. The destiny of the world depends upon the Father's response to this prayer, but this in turn depends upon the genuineness of our sincerity and the pureness of our hearts — upon our sanctity. St. Peter says the same thing: "What manner of persons ought ye to be in all holy conversation and godliness, looking for and hasting unto the coming of the day of God."

Jesus Christ, by the total gift of himself, has shown us the perfect priesthood. Image of all perfections, he is the one supreme Bishop and also the one supreme Layman, just as he is the one unique Saint. This is why his priestly prayer expresses the desire of all the saints, to glorify the Holy Trinity with one heart and soul, and to reunite all men around the one and only Chalice.

The Father's love for mankind waits for us to share in that joy which is no longer only of this world; already it initiates the Feast of the Kingdom.

At the very heart of existence there takes place the meeting, face to face, with the One who has already come; man is at last transformed into that which divine eternity makes of him, a saint. Then, when he has attained to the farthest extremity of the ultimately desirable, there is nothing more to be said except for the magnificent words of Evagrius, who thus describes the new man, "the man of the eighth day":

> "Separated from all, he is united to all;
> Impassible, yet of supreme sensitivity;
> Deified, he counts himself as the world's refuse,
> Above all he is happy,
> Divinely happy . . ."

Index